CW01018202

Rootzones, San

Top Dressing Materials

for Sports Turf

Stephen W Baker, BSc (Hons), PhD

STRI
St Ives Estate, Bingley,
West Yorkshire, BD16 1AU England
Tel: 01274 565131 Fax: 01274 561891
Email: info@stri.co.uk Website: www.stri.co.uk

Forewords

Selection of the correct soils, rootzone and top dressing materials is the most important factor in achieving high quality sports turf facilities. If the growing medium is of poor quality, healthy grass growth will inevitably be affected and the playing performance of the turf will suffer. Over the last twenty-five years, the Sports Turf Research Institute has had an extensive programme of research, funded primarily by the governing bodies of individual sports, to examine the most appropriate materials for construction and maintenance work. As a result of these studies, it is appropriate to outline guidelines for the selection of soils, rootzones and top dressing for the playing surfaces of a range of different sports, in particular winter games pitches, golf courses, bowling greens, cricket pitches and tennis courts. We believe that these guidelines will be of benefit not only to the users (greenkeepers, groundsmen, local authority staff and club officials) but also to the suppliers of rootzones and top dressings, most of who continually work to improve the quality of their materials and thus seek guidance on the implications of results from research that has been carried out.

The author wishes to express his grateful thanks to various members of staff for their comments on the guidelines and constructive criticism of the text. In particular I wish to thank Pat Reynard, Sharon Towler and Judith Beaumont for typing the manuscript, Anthony Woollacott for the preparation of the figures, and Ann Bentley for the design and layout in preparation for printing.

I am grateful to members of the sands, rootzone, top dressing and soil supply industries for support for this book and a list of contributors and their contact details are given in Appendix II. In particular, I wish to thank Topsport for their contribution to the printing and production costs for the book and to John Halfpenny, their General Manager, for his kind remarks on the use of the book by the sports turf industry.

Dr Stephen Baker
January 2006

Since the publication of the first edition of Sands for Sports Turf Construction and Maintenance it has become essential reading for all members of the sports turf construction industry. Grading curves have been committed to memory and dog-eared copies are to be found close to hand on many site office desks and on the bookshelves of all sports sand and rootzone suppliers. However, in the fifteen years between the two editions, the industry has undergone significant change with a great deal of research having been undertaken. As a result of these studies, this revised publication contains a more comprehensive summary of material selection requirements for the playing surfaces of a range of different sports.

In a market that is built upon natural materials, their correct selection and specification is critical. This book underlines the importance of material selection and the benefits of consistent material supply. As a Tarmac company, it is Topsport's aim to work to the most appropriate specifications recognised by the industry for the supply of high quality sands, gravels and rootzones. As such, Topsport are able to produce a varied selection of materials for the construction and maintenance of sports surfaces from over fifty quality assured locations nationwide.

We welcome the opportunity to support Stephen Baker and the STRI in this revision of the original sports sand book. It takes a great deal of time and effort to produce such a well researched document and express the findings in clear to understand text and figures. This publication will provide a comprehensive support manual to the natural sports surface architect, contractor and supplier for many years to come.

John Halfpenny
General Manager, Topsport
January 2006

Contents

Chapter 1

Introduction

The quality of a sports surface is always dependent on the soil or growing medium used in its construction. If the growing medium is of poor quality, matches are liable to be cancelled in adverse weather, playing standards will suffer and maintenance costs may increase. This has put a premium on high quality rootzones and top dressing materials.

The free-draining quality of sand and its availability at relatively low cost make it an ideal material for sports turf construction and maintenance, and its usage in the sports turf market has increased considerably in recent years. For example, a sand over gravel suspended water table pitch may require 1750 m^3 (2800 tonnes) of a sand-dominated rootzone mix. An eighteen hole golf course with an average of four bunkers per hole, each occupying an area of 50 m^2 would need 850-900 tonnes of sand to fill them, whilst a bowling club applying say 6 kg/m^2 of top dressing per year to the green could require up to 9.5 tonnes of sand-dominated top dressing material per year.

However, each of these particular operations requires a specific type of sand or sand-dominated medium. For example, the sand used in the rootzone layer of a soccer pitch would normally be finer than that of the sand used in golf bunkers or the top dressing of the bowling green. The lime content of a top dressing sand for a golf or bowling green can have a critical effect on grass species composition, the incidence of disease and weed invasion into the turf. The shape of the grains is relatively unimportant for a top dressing sand but has significant effects on the stacking angle, stability under foot and the incidence of ball plugging for golf bunkers.

For cricket or tennis, a sandy soil is unacceptable. It would be impossible to prepare the firm surfaces, with good ball bounce characteristics, needed for both sports. However, excessive clay content or high organic matter contents are also unacceptable. The relatively low drying rates of Britain's temperate, maritime climate mean that a cricket soil with more than 35% clay or a high organic matter content is impossible to dry out. Similarly, soils with a high organic matter content will not produce the dense surface layer needed for good bounce and pace, even if heavily rolled.

In other words, the choice of construction and top dressing materials is critical in all aspects of turfgrass management. The use of incorrectly specified materials or cheap, locally available products can have disastrous effects on the quality of a sports surface. There has been considerable research in recent years into the properties of rootzones, sands and top dressing material required for sports turf and the objectives of this work are to review the requirements for construction and maintenance procedures and to provide guidelines for the selection of materials for sports areas. The guidelines are intended primarily for use in the United Kingdom and other temperate climates where rainfall exceeds evapotranspiration for a significant part of the year. However, the general principles are applicable to many other parts of the world.

Chapter 2

Characterisation of Sands, Rootzones and Top Dressing

Characterising Sands

The characteristics of sands can be quantified in a number of ways. For sports turf, we need to know the size and uniformity of the sand grains and sometimes additional factors such as grain shape, hydraulic conductivity, shear strength and chemical composition of the sands. Various measurement techniques and associated indices have been developed: this section reviews the alternative methods and describes the approach used through the rest of the book.

Grain size distribution

The size distribution of sand materials is usually determined by shaking oven-dried sand material in a nest of sieves and then weighing the proportion retained on each sieve. Unfortunately, a variety of sieve sizes have been used by different groups within the sand industry. However, BS 410:2000 lists the following sequence of sizes with those in bold being the principal aperture sizes:

mm   **16.0**, 13.2, **11.2**, 9.5, **8.0**, 6.7, **5.6**, 4.75, **4.0**, 3.35, **2.8**, 2.36, **2.0**, 1.7, 1.4, 1.18, **1.0**

μm   850, **710**, 600, **500**, 425, **355**, 300, **250**, 212, **180**, 150, **125**, 106, **90**, 75, **63**, 53, **45**, 38, 32

It should be noted that 1 mm = 1000 μm (microns).

Various classifications of grain size have been used but the following classes are adopted in this book.

mm	μm	
8.0-4.0		Coarse gravel
4.0-2.0		Fine gravel
2.0-1.0		Very coarse sand
1.0-0.5	1000-500	Coarse sand
0.5-0.25	500-250	Medium sand
0.25-0.125	250-125	Fine sand
0.125-0.063	125-63	Very fine sand
0.063-0.002	63-2	Silt
<0.002	<2	Clay

The sieve test results can be expressed in a number of ways and in Table 1 three alternative descriptions of the same medium-fine sand are given.

TABLE 1. Various methods of showing particle size data for the same medium-fine sand.

Sieve size (mm)	% retained	Sieve size (mm)	% passing	Particle diameter (mm)	% in size range
1.0	0	1.0	100	1.0-0.5	3
0.5	3	0.5	97	0.5-0.25	64
0.25	64	0.25	33	0.25-0.125	32
0.125	32	0.125	1	0.125-0.063	1
0.063	1	0.063	0	<0.063	0
Pan	0				

In graphical form, results from the same sand are shown in Fig. 1. Traditionally, the size axis is based on a logarithmic scale.

There have also been attempts to describe the size of the sand by a single number. The most frequently used method is the D-number of a sand. This refers to the percentage of particles (by weight) less than a specified diameter, e.g. the D_{20} value could be viewed as a sieve size where 20% of the sand would pass through and 80% be retained. Many of the performance characteristics relate to the D_{10} and D_{20} parameters of a sand. The mid-particle diameter (D_{50}) is also sometimes used. For the sand in Fig. 1, the D_{10}, D_{20} and D_{50} values would be 0.19, 0.22 and 0.30 mm respectively.

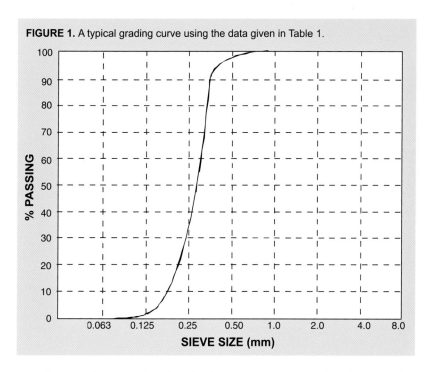

FIGURE 1. A typical grading curve using the data given in Table 1.

Sometimes an AFS (American Foundry Society) number is used and this number increases as the sand gets finer. The AFS number appears as part of the description of a number of sands used in the sports industry, e.g. Mansil 55 is a medium-fine material whereas Chelford 35 sand is a medium to medium-coarse material. AFS numbers of about 25 to 60 define the main range of sands used in the sports industry, except for certain coarser materials used primarily as blinding layers.

Uniformity of the size distribution

The uniformity of the grains has an important influence on the density to which the sand will pack and the stability of the material. It is therefore important to be able to characterise grain uniformity. The usual approach is to use a gradation index or coefficient of uniformity, which expresses the size ratio of the larger to smaller grains. For example, the D_{90}/D_{10} gradation index is obtained by dividing the D_{90} value (i.e. a diameter where 90% of the grains are smaller) by the D_{10} value (i.e. the diameter where only 10% of the grains are smaller). In the example shown in Fig. 2, both sands have the same mid-particle diameter (D_{50} = 0.3 mm) but have very different distributions. Sand A is relatively uniform so the D_{90} value (in this case 0.38 mm) is not that much larger than the D_{10} value (0.19 mm) giving a relatively low gradation index of 0.38/0.19 = 2.0. On the other hand, sand B has a wide spread of particles and the D_{90} value (2.9 mm) is therefore substantially larger than the D_{10} figure (0.15 mm). The gradation index in this case is therefore 2.9/0.15 = 19.3.

FIGURE 2. Grading curves of two sands. Sand A has a uniform particle size distribution, whilst Sand B has a wide spread of particles.

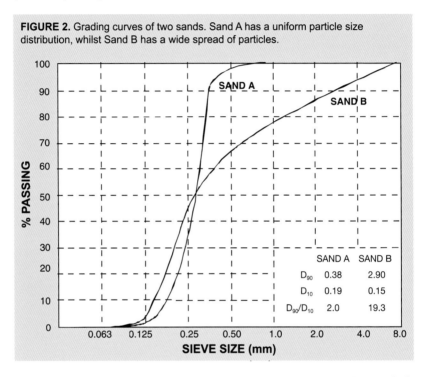

The D_{90}/D_{10} value is not the only gradation index currently in use; others include D_{95}/D_5 and D_{60}/D_{10}. They are, however, closely related and Table 2, derived from a total of 118 sands, shows the relationships between the three indices.

TABLE 2. Relationship between D_{90}/D_{10} gradation index and other indices commonly in use.

Regression equation	r	Significant level
$\log_{10}(D_{90}/D_{10}) = 0.809 \log_{10}(D_{95}/D_5) - 0.05$	0.95	P<0.0001
$\log_{10}(D_{90}/D_{10}) = 1.752 \log_{10}(D_{60}/D_{10}) + 0.078$	0.81	P<0.0001

Various preferred limits have been suggested for the different indices of uniformity. For top dressing and construction sands, these are listed in Table 3 and, for comparative purposes, are also converted into a corresponding D_{90}/D_{10} gradation index using the equations given in Table 2. An average of these values would suggest that the D_{90} should be at most eight times larger than the D_{10} value if the sand is to be sufficiently uniform for sports turf usage.

TABLE 3. Published recommendations for particle uniformity for sports turf sands.

Authors	Index	Limits	Equivalent D_{90}/D_{10} index
Adams et al. (1971)	D_{90}/D_{10}	c. 2.5	c. 2.5
Adams (1982)	D_{90}/D_{10}	6-12	6-12
Bingaman & Kohnke (1970)	D_{95}/D_5	2-6	1.6-3.4
Blake (1980)	D_{60}/D_{10}	<4	<13.6

Particle shape

Two main parameters are generally used to describe the shape of sand grains. The sphericity of the grain indicates its closeness to a perfect sphere with highly elongated grains being described as having low sphericity. A snooker ball would therefore have high sphericity whereas a rugby ball would have low sphericity. The angularity of the grains relates more to the microscale roughness of the grain's surface, with sands ranging from well rounded to highly angular. The two components of sphericity and angularity are usually derived by examining the grains under a microscope (magnification to x 25) and comparing the shape with standard charts (e.g. Fig. 3). Where necessary, numerical indices can be used to express the characteristics of sphericity and angularity.

Measurement of the Physical Properties of Soils, Rootzones and Top Dressing

Soils and top dressing mixes

Soil materials are normally characterised in terms of their soil texture and organic matter content. Texture is defined by the proportions of sand, silt and clay. Silt and clay are usually determined by sedimentation, a process that relies on the fact that particles of different sizes will settle in water at different

FIGURE 3. Chart showing the angularity and sphericity of sand grains.

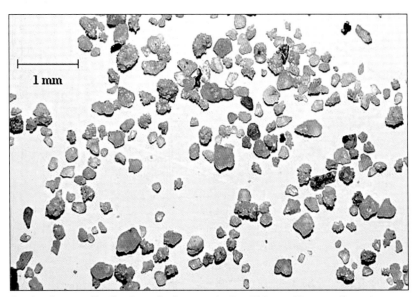

Sand under magnification for grain shape evaluation. This sand has a uniform size distribution with the majority of grains 0.25-0.5 mm diameter. Grains are predominantly sub-angular to angular with medium sphericity.

rates. The larger and therefore heavier sand particles (0.063-2.0 mm) will sink more quickly than silt particles (0.002-0.063 mm), which in turn sink faster than the very fine clay particles (<0.002 mm). Various pre-treatments are needed to remove organic matter content and chemical bonding between particles. Sedimentation rates can be measured either by taking pipette samples or by measuring the density of the suspension using a hydrometer at specified times that depend on temperature. After washing, the sand component is divided into the different size fractions by sieving.

Sedimentation and sieving for particle size analysis of rootzone mixes.

Organic matter content is usually measured by loss on ignition. Oven-dried material is placed in a furnace (e.g. at temperatures of 360° C or 400° C depending on the test method specified) and the organic matter content is assumed to be equivalent to the loss of weight. Organic matter content can also be measured chemically, for example using the Walkley-Black method based on breakdown of the organic matter using potassium dichromate.

Rootzone mixes

The objective of preparing sand-dominated rootzone mixes is to create a growing medium which gives good drainage and will support healthy grass growth even when it is heavily compacted by players and maintenance equipment. As well as particle size and organic matter content, the physical properties of rootzone mixes after compaction are a valuable guide to the future performance of the selected material.

The normal procedure is to place the rootzone material in a metal cylinder, to adjust moisture content to a range where maximum compaction is likely to occur, then to compact the mix with a specified number of blows of a falling weight. Four main properties are measured:

- **Hydraulic conductivity** (also referred to as Ksat, i.e. saturated hydraulic conductivity and percolation rate). This parameter gives an indication of rates of water flow through the rootzone medium.

Measurement of saturated hydraulic conductivity in the STRI laboratory.

- **Total porosity.** This is the volume not occupied by solid matter, in other words an indication of the spaces between particles of mineral and organic matter.

- **Air-filled porosity.** This component of total porosity is the volume of larger pores normally occupied by air after drainage by gravity.

- **Capillary porosity.** This component of total porosity is the volume of finer pores normally occupied by water after drainage by gravity.

Air-filled porosity and capillary porosity are normally measured at a specified tension or suction, e.g. 30 cm or 40 cm tension, depending on the test method selected.

For golf rootzones, testing is usually carried out in accordance with protocols developed by the United States Golf Association and written as ASTM (American Society for Testing and Materials) standards.

For winter games pitches, the STRI normally uses a similar method but with larger cylinders (100 mm diameter), a lower compaction rate (18.9 kJ/m^2) and a tension of 40 cm for air-filled porosity and capillary porosity measurements.

Cricket and tennis soils

Silt, clay and organic matter content are routinely measured in the assessment of cricket and tennis soils. However, binding strength and shrinkage properties are also important. These can be determined from a moulded ball (a motty) of approximately 25 mm initial diameter. These are moulded when moist to breakdown any soil structure, then allowed to dry for four days. Shrinkage is assessed from the change in volume of each motty before and after drying. Binding strength is determined by applying a force downwards onto the motty until it shatters. Binding strength in kilograms is recorded.

Preparation of soil motties for testing the binding strength and shrinkage of cricket and tennis soils.

Chemical Properties

There are a range of techniques available to measure the pH, lime and plant nutrient content of sands and soils. For sports turf, the most important aspect is the lime content of the sands and soils as this will affect the acidity (pH) of the turf. The techniques used at the Sports Turf Research Institute are:

- **pH:** A 20 ml volume of sand or soil is mixed with 20 ml distilled water. After allowing the material to stand for 1 hour, the pH of the mixture is measured electrometrically using a pH electrode.

- **Lime content:** The calcium carbonate content can be measured using an adaptation of a gravimetric method used for soils. The loss in weight after the addition of 40 ml 3M hydrochloric acid to a 10 g sample is measured accurately to 0.1 mg. This is compared to a blank run in which de-ionised water is substituted for the hydrochloric acid. The difference in weight loss can be attributed to carbon dioxide from any calcium carbonate present in the sand or soil.

A good indication of lime content can, however, be obtained by adding 10% hydrochloric acid or warm vinegar (acetic acid) to the material and observing the reaction. The degree of bubble formation can be interpreted from Table 4.

The pH of sands is usually fairly difficult to interpret because of the low exchange capacity of the sand material and it is felt that, for unamended sands, lime content is usually a better indicator of the potential effect on turf performance.

TABLE 4. Calcium carbonate contents (from Soil Survey 1974).

CaCO$_3$ %	Audible effects (when held close to ear)	Visible effects
0.1	None	None
0.5	Faintly increasing to slightly audible	None
1.0	Faintly increasing to moderately audible	Slight effervescence confined to individual grains, just visible
2.0	Moderately to distinctly audible; heard away from ear	Slightly more general effervescence visible on close inspection
5.0	Easily audible	Moderate effervescence; obvious bubbles up to 3 mm diameter
10.0	Easily audible	General strong effervescence; ubiquitous bubbles to 7 mm diameter; easily seen

Chapter 3

Sources and Properties of Sand

Source of Sand Material

Sands are formed by the breakdown of crystalline igneous and metamorphic rocks or from existing sandstone rock materials. This breakdown is brought about by both physical and chemical agencies. Physical breakdown is caused by frost, rain and wind whilst chemical weathering is associated with changes in mineral composition of the rock material. The nature of the parent rock material has an important influence on sand materials. For example, with granite the quartz particles are resistant to chemical decomposition but the feldspars and mica can break down more readily. Micas have a plate-like structure and therefore have a large surface area for chemical activity. Furthermore, they can be fairly brittle and subject to physical breakdown. Depending on the duration and intensity of chemical weathering, the feldspar will gradually be removed but some sands still have 20% feldspar material. Other heavy minerals may also be present depending on the state of chemical decomposition. However, silica is the dominant material in most sands.

Transportation processes also have a major influence on sand characteristics. Glacial and fluvio-glacial sands are generally poorly sorted, i.e. have a wide range of particle sizes and tend to have angular grains. Windblown sands are typically uniform in size and more rounded, whilst transport and deposition of sand by water tends to separate the sand into distinct size categories and the rubbing together of the particles causes rounding.

Sand is used in a wide range of industries with, of course, sands for sports turf forming only a fraction of the extracted sand materials. The principal uses for sand are in building industries, foundries and glassmaking, whilst sands are also used for sewage and water filtration, horticulture and ceramics. This means that there is a wide range of potential sources of sand materials including:

(a) **Sand quarries.** Natural deposits of sand materials which can be excavated.
(b) **Dune sands.** However, many of these sands are no longer available because of environmental considerations.

(c) **River-washed sands.**

(d) **Estuarine and sea-dredged sands.**

(e) **Sandstone rock materials.** These include weakly cemented materials but which often have a high clay content, e.g. from the Bunter Sandstone. Other rocksands are extracted from harder rock materials by crushing and milling, e.g. from Millstone Grit in Staffordshire and the Scottish rocksands between Falkirk and Glasgow.

(f) **Sand waste from China clay extraction.**

(g) **Sands derived from recycled glass.** The glass is crushed and milled, then processed to give specific size fractions.

Sands from certain sources can be used without further processing, others may undergo a sequence of washing, sieving or screening and hydrosizing to achieve a uniform, clay-free product. Some of the rocksands may be washed or leached in hot acid principally to remove iron oxides.

Sand deposits date from various periods in the geological timescale. For example, the band of sands through Kent to Norfolk, including the Leighton Buzzard and Redhill/Reigate sands, date from the Lower Cretaceous (65-135 million years ago), while the extensive fluvio-glacial deposits around Chelford and Congleton in Cheshire date from the Pleistocene (0.1-2 million years ago). River and dune sand materials are, of course, of much more recent origin.

The Physical Behaviour of Sand

The size, uniformity and shape of sand particles control the physical behaviour of the material. In selecting sands for sports turf, it is important to be able to define the attributes required from the surface, e.g. drainage rate, water retention or stability, and to select a size range that most closely satisfies these criteria. In rootzone mixes or top dressings, the physical properties of the sand are often modified by the addition of sandy soil or an organic amendment. However, the characteristics of the sand usually have a major influence on the mix that is produced.

Effect of grain size

Grain size has major effects on water movement, water retention and the amount of air-filled pore space in sands and rootzone mixes. As an example,

Fig. 4 gives data from an STRI study in which the effects of different sands were examined for three rootzone mixes: 75/25 sand/peat, 85/15 sand/organic-rich fensoil and 80/20 sand/sandy loam soil. Rootzone mixes based on sands with a D_{20} of 0.1 mm had hydraulic conductivity rates about one-fifth of those of mixes with coarser sands with a D_{20} of 0.5 mm. The particle size of the sand strongly influenced the balance between finer capillary pores that are important for water retention and the larger air-filled pores that are important for air exchange around the roots of the grass plant. For example, with finer sands (D_{20} = 0.1 mm), there was typically 10% air-filled pore space and 35% capillary pore space. In contrast, for the coarser sands (D_{20} = 0.5 mm), there was typically 30% air-filled pore space and 15% capillary porosity.

Sand selection is a balance between the needs of good drainage and aeration on the one hand and reasonable moisture retention on the other, to avoid a droughty mix with rapid nutrient leaching. For the mixes in question, a D_{20} value between about 0.2 mm and 0.4 mm would give a good compromise for a rootzone for a golf or bowling green.

Relationships of grain size to movement of sands by wind are of particular importance in bunker sands as this will regulate losses of sand by windblow. It can also be important during construction work where stockpiles of sand have been known to disappear in windy conditions and surface levels of sand constructions can be disrupted in high winds if adequate moisture is not applied before the seedlings develop.

A final physical property influenced by grain size is the stability of the sand material. This is important, for example, in sand-based rootzones for winter games as it influences the amount of grip available for the players. It can also be significant in bunker sands because poor footholds and plugging of balls can be a problem in unstable sands. Coarser sands are less stable for two reasons: [i] inter-particle friction is greater for finer sands because of the increased contact area between particles, [ii] fine sands are more moisture retentive and it is under dry conditions that stability problems become more acute.

Uniformity of particles

The uniformity of the sand particles controls the physical nature of the pore space after compaction. Uniform rounded grains packed to their maximum

FIGURE 4. The effect of sand particle size on selected physical properties of rootzone mixes (data from Zhang & Baker 1999).

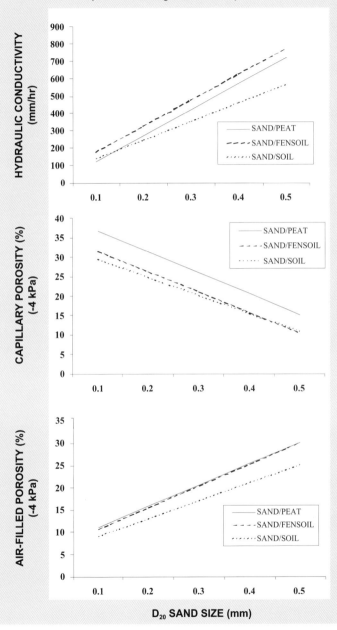

density will give approximately 60% solid matter and therefore 40% pore space. However, sand grains of approximately 40% of the size of the primary particles would fit into the gaps between the large sand grains and reduce the pore space further (Fig. 5). Table 5 shows the effect of sand uniformity on total porosity and the proportions of fine and larger pores for compacted sand. In all cases the mid-particle diameter was the same (0.38 mm), however sand A had 80% of material in the medium sand size category (0.25-0.5 mm) whereas

FIGURE 5. The effect on sand uniformity on particle interpacking.

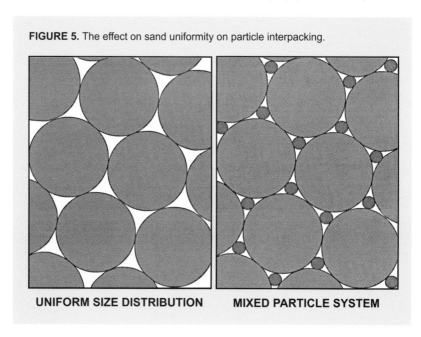

UNIFORM SIZE DISTRIBUTION   MIXED PARTICLE SYSTEM

TABLE 5. Effect of particle uniformity on total porosity and pore space of compacted sand.

	Sand size (mm)[†]								
VFS	FS	MS	CS	VCS	Mid particle diameter	Gradation index	Total porosity	Pores >37 μm	Pores <37 μm
0.063-0.125	0.125-0.25	0.25-0.5	0.5-1.0	1.0-2.0	D_{50} (mm)	D_{90}/D_{10}	(%)	(%)	(%)
A	0	10	80	10	0	0.38	2.0	37.0	25.2	11.8
B	0	30	40	30	0	0.38	5.0	35.5	16.3	19.5
C	10	20	40	20	10	0.38	8.0	33.6	10.6	23.0

[†] Sand sizes: VFS = very fine sand, FS = fine sand, MS = medium sand, CS = coarse sand, VCS = very coarse sand.

sand C had a very wide spread of particles (0.063-2.0 mm). After compaction sand A had 37.0% pore space with 25.2% pore space greater than 37 μm. Sand C had only 33.6% pore space and just 10.5% pore space greater than 37 μm. There were other effects of uniformity : bulk density was 1.67, 1.72 and 1.75 g/cc respectively for sands A, B and C while corresponding figures for hydraulic conductivity were 863, 671 and 273 mm/hr.

The uniformity of sands also affects their stability. For example, Fig. 6 shows the shear strength of three types of rootzone in relation to gradation index, with shear strength increasing with a greater spread of particles. In rootzone mixes, grass cover also contributes to shear strength so very uniform materials are not necessarily a major problem unless the sand is coarse and dries out. However in bunker sands very uniform materials can cause problems of stability.

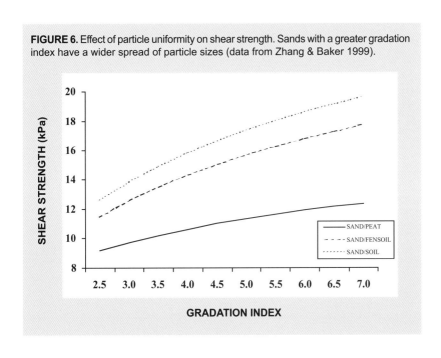

FIGURE 6. Effect of particle uniformity on shear strength. Sands with a greater gradation index have a wider spread of particle sizes (data from Zhang & Baker 1999).

Effect of grain shape

For most construction and maintenance purposes, the effect of grain shape is relatively small compared to the importance of grain size and uniformity. There are two counteracting factors: theoretically angular grains of the same size distribution could pack more tightly than rounded ones if the compaction forces are high because the angular protrusions can fit into the void spaces between adjacent grains. However, inter-particle friction is greater for angular particles and it is rare, therefore, that maximum packing densities are attained. Certainly, in both laboratory studies and field trials, we have found that mixes containing either more rounded grains and or more elongated grains had lower values of total porosity. Conversely, hydraulic conductivity and air-filled pore space were greater when the sand contained either angular or spherical particles.

Particle shape does have some influence on the stability of sand. For example, STRI studies have shown that a greater proportion of angular grains in the sand component increased the shear strength of sand-soil mixes. Particle shape can be particularly important in sands for golf bunkers where more angular grains are likely to contribute to better footing and reduce the risk of ball plugging. Studies of bunker sands at the STRI have shown that the angle of the sand at the bunker face can also be greater for angular sands, i.e. around 34° for a sub-angular material compared to 31° for a sand with rounded grains.

The effects of the particle size distribution is usually much greater than the effect of grain shape and this makes it hard to justify specifying grain shape as a criterion in sand selection. However, sub-rounded to sub-angular sands may be best for winter games pitches where stability is more of a problem. On golf and bowling greens, there has been some evidence of an unstable surface during grass establishment if coarse, well-rounded grains are dominant, as this may cause tracking lines to develop where maintenance equipment is used. There has also been some evidence of root abrasion when sands are dominated by very angular particles. Rounded to sub-angular grains are likely to be the most suitable shape. More angular materials are usually preferred in golf bunkers.

Chemical Properties of Sand

Although silica is the dominant constituent of sands, other chemical compounds may also be present and, in particular, contents of Al_2O_3, Fe_2O_5, K_2O and $CaCO_3$, can often exceed 1%. In industrial usage, high concentrations of various impurities can be important, e.g. iron can affect a sand's suitability for glass manufacture. For turf areas, the most important factor is undoubtedly lime content.

Lime content

The lime content of a sand will strongly influence the acidity of the turf with additions of lime increasing alkalinity, i.e. raising the pH. This is particularly important on fine turf areas where the fescue and bent grasses are more closely adapted to pH values of around 4.5-5.5. Increased lime content will increase the competitiveness of annual meadow-grass and many broad-leaved weeds. Furthermore, a high pH will encourage earthworm activity. Hence casting will increase and turf diseases such as take-all patch (*Gaeumannomyces graminis*) are more common when high concentrations of lime are present. On winter games pitches, the grasses are more tolerant of higher pH (e.g. perennial ryegrass has pH optimum of about 6.0-7.5). However, the addition of a lime rich sand can cause a considerable increase in earthworm casting and, in the absence of pesticides that have long term control of earthworm activity, the use of sands with a low lime content is essential on most sites.

For most applications on sports turf areas the lime content of any sand, rootzone or top dressing should be below 0.5%. On winter games pitches with fairly acid soils, top dressing sands with a lime content up to 2% might be acceptable.

Salt content

Some sands, most notably dredged sea sands, can contain high salt contents. These must be well washed before use, particularly when applied to fine turf. Salt content is normally measured in terms of electrical conductivity on an extract of the sand, with conductivity increasing as salt content increases. A conductivity value less than 6 dS/m (mS/cm) on a water saturated sand extract is appropriate for use on established turf, although when seeding is to take place values below 3 dS/m are preferred. If a saturated calcium sulphate sand extract were used, a conductivity value in the range 1.9 to 2.8 dS/m would be appropriate.

Other plant nutrients

With silica being the dominant component of sands, it is inevitable that sands are relatively inert with respect to the major plant nutrients. Sands do not contain nitrogen and, certainly in Britain, phosphate and potassium contents are generally very low. However, there is wide variation with, for example, relatively high contents of potassium occurring in areas of granite or basalt rocks where the sand materials are relatively young and have not therefore undergone prolonged chemical weathering.

However, sands may well contain adequate contents of the minor plant nutrients. Table 6 shows the results of a survey of 62 sands, most of which have been applied to sports turf areas. Virtually all the sands had adequate contents of calcium and iron and many had sufficient reserves of magnesium and copper. Most sand-dominated rootzones containing relatively high concentrations of soil or an organic amendment will have the full range of essential micro-nutrients. However, on very sandy rootzones, it may be advisable to add the entire range of micronutrients which are needed by the grass plant, e.g. as fritted trace element.

TABLE 6. Chemical analysis of sands for sports turf (from Lawson & Baker 1987).

Chemical property	Unit	Range of values		% satisfying published requirements for
		Minimum	Maximum	plant growth
pH		4.5	9.3	Not applicable
Calcium carbonate	%	0	46	Not applicable
Phosphate	mg/l	0	14	5
Potassium	mg/l	2	230	5
Magnesium	mg/l	1	168	44
Calcium	mg/l	23	100	100
Iron	mg/l	1	138	97
Copper	mg/l	1	11	39

Chapter 4
Sands and Sand-dominated Root-zones in Sports Turf Construction

Introduction

Sand-dominated rootzones are regularly used in the construction of new sports pitches, golf greens and bowling greens because existing soils at many sites would have inadequate drainage under conditions of moderate or heavy wear. Apart from those soils that are naturally sandy in texture, most soils depend on aggregation to create a system of large pores for adequate drainage and aeration. This aggregation is brought about by physical and chemical processes associated particularly with the clay and organic matter fractions. It is the large soil pores between the aggregates which remain air-filled at field capacity and which are responsible for rapid drainage of the soil. If the soil is compacted, these larger pores are diminished and the soil becomes poor draining and waterlogged. On most natural soils used for sports turf, it is the inability of the compacted surface layer to transmit rainfall rapidly from the surface which causes poor playing conditions or cancellation of games.

Sand-based materials, on the other hand, do not rely on structure for drainage. Instead there is a stable network of pores between the sand grains and, as long as the sand is chosen carefully with respect to its size and uniformity, this can provide a growing medium with high rates of drainage and adequate aeration for plant growth.

The purpose of this chapter is to examine how sand, or sand-dominated materials, can be used to improve the quality of sports turf. Three main situations are considered, i.e. winter games pitches, fine turf areas and golf bunkers.

Winter Games Pitches

The principal types of construction for winter games pitches (i.e. soccer, Rugby and hockey) range from the native soil with a series of pipe drains through slit drainage to sand-dominated rootzones.

Pipe drained pitches

Pipe drained pitches, and indeed those with no drains at all, rely on soil structure for water to pass through the surface layer. This may be perfectly adequate if the pitch is lightly used and if it is possible to cancel games in wet weather but, as discussed above, if the soil surface becomes smeared and compacted, water transmission rates decline rapidly and even if the pipe drains are closely spaced, say 5 m apart, water will not reach them quickly enough to improve the quality of the surface.

Slit drained pitches

One solution to compaction in the surface is to install a series of permeable bands at close centres connecting the turf surface to the gravel backfill of the drains (Fig. 7). These slit drains are usually filled with sand or sand over gravel. Three main categories of slit drainage can be recognised:

FIGURE 7. The layout of a typical slit drainage system with excavated slits filled with sand and gravel.

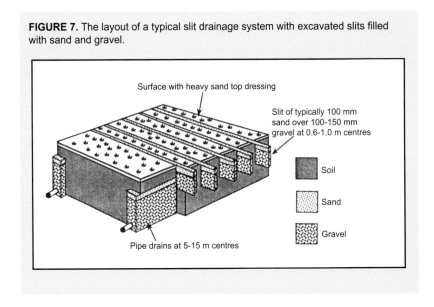

(a) Excavated slits, where soil is excavated with a trenching machine and the spoil is removed, leaving channels typically 50-75 mm in width. These channels are filled with either sand or a layer of sand over a suitable drainage aggregate.

(b) Sand or gravel banding, where deep bands of sand (or sometimes a fine gravel) typically 15-20 mm in width run from the surface either into the under-drainage or into more permeable soil horizons. No soil excavation takes place, but instead a cutting blade forces the soil apart and sand or gravel is added to the resulting fissure.

Construction of slit drains: excavated slits (top), installation of sand banding (bottom).

(c)   Surface grooving, where shallow slits are inserted to a depth of 75-100 mm. The principal use is to restore continuity between the soil surface and existing slits that have been capped by soil.

Some slit drainage schemes will consist of combinations of the different types of slit with the objective of obtaining a close spacing of slits at the surface. It is important that slits are at relatively close centres otherwise water will accumulate in the areas of soil between the slits. A spacing of 1 m is considered to be about the maximum to prevent ponding whilst for surface grooving the spacing is generally as close as 0.2 m.

The design of a slit drainage system must allow for the layout of the underlying pipe drainage system, surface gradients, the dimensions of the slits, the permeability of the soil and the slit materials, likely rainfall intensities and the consequences of the design rainfall being exceeded.

The success of a slit drainage scheme is very dependent on subsequent sand top dressing. If the slits become capped by soil material, their effectiveness for water transmission is reduced considerably. Top dressing requirements are discussed in more detail in Chapter 6.

Soil amelioration and sand-dominated rootzones

Instead of adding vertical bands of permeable material to bypass compacted, poor-draining soil, an alternative is to modify the rootzone so that it is free-draining even after the compacting effects of play. Sufficient quantities of a uniform sand must be added to the soil so that a permanent network of large pores is formed between the sand grains. The amount of sand is critical and, for example, Fig. 8 shows the effect of different mixing rates with a sandy loam soil on various aspects of turf performance. After three seasons of simulated wear, infiltration rates were still over 400 mm/h on the pure sand (0:1) treatment, 11 mm/h for the mix of 2 parts sand:1 part soil and only 4 mm/h on the mix containing 1 part sand:1 part soil. The low infiltration rates on the 1:1 mixes meant that standing water was a severe problem and during the playing season when monitoring took place, ponding was recorded on 20% of assessment dates. This compared to a 4% incidence of surface water on the 2:1 mixes and the sand plots were effectively free from ponding.

FIGURE 8. The effect of sand content on infiltration rates, ground cover and firmness of football turf receiving artificial wear. The 1:1, 1:2 and 0:1 (pure sand) materials had sand contents of 86, 90 and 100% respectively (adapted from Baker 1988 and Baker *et al.* 1988).

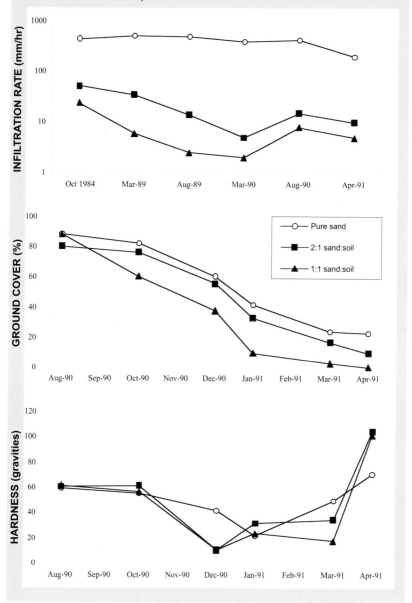

Spreading the sand-dominated rootzone during the construction of a soccer pitch.

The unfavourable physical conditions meant that grass cover was lost more quickly on the 1:1 mixes and these mixes also gave a poor quality surface for play. During the playing season the 1:1 mixes had an unacceptably soft surface (hardness values <10 N m) on over 11% of sampling occasions. This compares excessively soft conditions only 1% of the time for the 2 sand:1 soil mixes and never for the pure sand rootzones.

Adding too little sand in amelioration work can sometimes produce worse results than just using the soil without addition of sand. This can arise because soil structure is lost during the mixing process. Instead a critical threshold of sand is required before there is any significant improvement in the soil physical properties of the mix. This threshold is reached when the sand grains begin to abut with adjacent grains. Inadequate sand contents probably account for the rather limited success of amelioration projects in the past: an STRI drainage survey in the early 1980s for instance found that over 40% of sand ameliorated pitches still had inadequate drainage.

Pipe drains only (muddy)	Sand over gravel	Slit drained (sand top)	Slit drained (no sand top)
Sand over gravel	Pipe drains only (muddy)	Sand carpet	
Bank			

The effect of construction type on the qualtiy of turf after four months of simulated soccer-type wear. Note the contrast between the topsoil with pipe drainage and the sand rootzones.

STRI trial on golf green rootzone materials.

As a minimum requirement for amelioration work it is suggested that sufficient quantities of a clean, uniform sand should be added to dilute the finer fractions to:

Clay   (particles <0.002 mm diameter)   <4%
Silt + clay   (particles <0.063 mm diameter)   <8%
Fines   (particles <0.125 mm diameter)   <15%

Heavier soils will, of course, require more sand. For example, to meet the requirements above, a sandy loam soil with an initial content of 15% clay and 20% silt would require 3 parts of sand for each volume of soil, whilst a clay loam soil, initially with 25% clay and 30% silt, would require a mix of 5.5 parts sand to 1 part of soil. Whilst it may be possible to obtain a reasonable mix with a 3:1 sand:soil ratio, it is doubtful whether a 5.5:1 mix could be mixed accurately, even if such a clay rich soil was in a sufficiently friable state for mixing.

Most good quality rootzone mixes are now prepared off-site by specialist suppliers. They are able to import sandy textured soils as the amendment material, and have the advantages of screening facilities to remove stone and gravel and proper blending equipment to ensure a homogeneous rootzone and a high level of quality control. For high quality pitches it is also common practice to reinforce the rootzone with a variety of plastic fibres, mainly to improve the stability of the surface. The fibres can be incorporated into the rootzone by a number of methods, including:

i)   mixing into the rootzone during the blending process before transport to site,
ii) installation in the form of a carpet with a biodegradable backing into which rootzone material is worked,
iii) punching into the rootzone after grass has been established.

Projects involving blends of sand and soil need detailed laboratory testing to establish an optimum rootzone mix. This would normally involve the measurement of the hydraulic conductivity and air-filled/capillary porosity of the proposed rootzone materials after compaction, as well as optimising its particle size distribution.

Pure sand rootzones

Pure sand rootzones have sometimes been used for winter games pitches to provide high drainage rates and to remove the need for precise blending of sand and soil. They are more likely to be successful in wetter parts of the country (e.g. Northern Ireland), especially if usage is relatively light. However, use of pure sand creates higher demands in terms of irrigation and fertiliser management. Furthermore, if ground cover is lost through wear and the surface dries out, there can be severe problems of surface stability, especially if the sand grading is too coarse. This creates excessive demands on maintenance, particularly watering, rolling and the reinstatement of line markings. For this reason, pure sand rootzones are now rarely specified in the United Kingdom.

Construction profiles and associated costs

There are three main ways in which sand can be used in the construction of winter games pitches.

(a) For constructions with either a good quality natural soil or a limited budget, a thin layer of sand (e.g. 20-25 mm) may be worked into the immediate surface to protect the soil from smearing and provide a firmer surface layer.

(b) Sand carpet—typically 100-150 mm of sand or sand-dominated rootzone over the native soil which is intensively drained by pipe drains and slit (Fig. 9).

(c) Suspended water table—usually 300 mm of the rootzone material over a 50 mm blinding layer and a gravel drainage carpet of 100-150 mm. In many cases the upper 150 mm of the rootzone is a sand/soil blend with a compatible sand forming the lower half of the rootzone (Fig. 10).

FIGURE 9. Layout of a typical sand carpet construction.

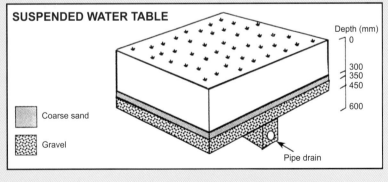

SAND CARPET

Slits typically at 1.0-1.5 m centres

Depth (mm)
0
100

600

Soil

Fine sand

Coarse sand

Gravel

Pipe drains at 5-15 m centres

FIGURE 10. Layout of a typical suspended water table construction with a three-layered system of rootzone, blinding layer and drainage carpet.

SUSPENDED WATER TABLE

Depth (mm)
0

300
350
450

600

Coarse sand

Gravel

Pipe drain

A pitch with an intensive system of pipe drains at say 5 m centres with a layer of sand worked into the upper 10 mm of the soil profile may cost £25,000-30,000. Its success is likely to be very dependent on the quality of the native soil and, if necessary, a slit drainage system costing a further £25,000 may be needed. The sand carpet pitches cost around £100,000, including a pop-up irrigation system. Since the grass roots can penetrate into the underlying soil, this type of construction is usually less sensitive in its requirements for irrigation and fertiliser. However, the construction work must be carried out with extreme care because compaction of the soil or smearing of soil over the drainage slits can impair the subsequent efficiency of a sand carpet pitch.

A basic suspended water table pitch costs around £400,000 including irrigation, but the cost would increase to £600,000 with reinforced rootzone and an undersoil heating system. They have the advantage of very high drainage rates and this means that play is guaranteed under any rainfall conditions. The gravel carpet is important in that it ensures drainage is not restricted during wet weather because of low permeability of the sub-base. However, it also helps conserve moisture in dry conditions because water will not flow downward from the rootzone sand into the gravel because of the abrupt change in pore sizes of the two materials. However, this type of construction will usually show drought stress more quickly than a sand carpet pitch and careful management of the fertiliser is also more critical.

Fine Turf Areas

Golf greens

It is generally agreed that the game of golf originated in Scotland, typically on the areas of medium-fine dune sand which are found along the east coast. Later, inland courses were developed using the native soils at the site and although many were of high quality, an increase in the popularity of golf and the amount of leisure time (giving more rounds per course each year) gradually exposed those courses where the native soil did not have adequate drainage. Thus, for areas receiving high wear, particularly golf greens and to a lesser extent tees, the use of sand in construction has increased rapidly in the last thirty-five years.

Research work financed by the United States Golf Association (USGA) throughout the 1950s and early 1960s was paramount in establishing the use of sand

Spreading a golf green rootzone over a gravel drainage layer.

as a building material for golf greens. In 1960, this work led to a USGA Green Section Staff publication outlining specifications for green construction. The recommendations have been revised a number of times, most recently in 2004. The current USGA recommendations for a method of putting green construction include the following requirements:

(a)   Either a two layered or a three layered construction can be used. Both include a 300 mm deep rootzone layer. In the two layered system this is placed on a relatively fine gravel drainage layer with minimum thickness of 100 mm (Fig. 11). There are specified bridging criteria to ensure that rootzone material does not migrate downwards into the underlying gravel. For the three layered system an intermediate layer of 1-4 mm grit of 50-100 mm thickness is placed over a coarser gravel, which has at least 65% of particles between 6-9 mm diameter.

(b)   The rootzone mix should be dominated by sand but amended with, for example, organic matter or a sandy textured soil. There should be at least 60% of particles between 0.25-1.0 mm diameter with no more than 3% clay, no more than 5% silt and no more than 3% fine gravel (>2 mm), indeed preferably none.

(c) There are strict requirements for the physical performance of the root-zone mix including total porosity 35-55%, air-filled porosity 15-30%, capillary porosity 15-25%, saturated hydraulic conductivity of at least 150 mm/h.

FIGURE 11. Typical construction of a suspended water table golf green. Where a coarse gravel is used, a 50 mm thick intermediate layer may be needed.

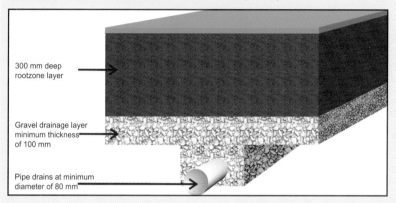

300 mm deep rootzone layer

Gravel drainage layer minimum thickness of 100 mm

Pipe drains at minimum diameter of 80 mm

In the United Kingdom, a number of studies at the STRI have examined the performance of different rootzones and construction profiles for golf greens. This has led to a modification of the USGA method that is considered to be more appropriate for conditions in the United Kingdom. More specific details are given in Chapter 8.

As an alternative to a mix of sand plus an amendment material over a gravel base, pure sand constructions have also been used. For example, the University of California have advocated sand constructions with 300 mm of sand over the native soil. The sand is chosen to have 85-95% of its particles between 0.1-1.0 mm diameter, with over 60% between 0.25-0.5 mm diameter. No gravel drainage layer is used but pipe drains are usually added at approximately 3 m centres. However, where the underlying soil takes water at over 6-12 mm/h, a pipe system may not be necessary if heavy rain and excessive irrigation are not a problem.

Similar constructions based on sand-dominated rootzones are widely used in the Netherlands. These typically have a 150-200 mm deep surface layer, usually incorporating an organic amendment, e.g. heather compost, over a pure sand base of typically 250-300 mm depth. Pipe drainage is usually installed at the base of the sand.

In Britain, sand-soil rootzone mixes or blends of sand with an organic matter source have generally been favoured to pure sand constructions because they give a less hard surface with lower management requirements in terms of nutrition and irrigation than pure sand greens. Sand-soil mixes or blends of sand and organic material must be to a high technical specification to ensure proper performance.

Bowling greens

Specifications for bowling greens closely follow those for golf green construction with sand-soil mixes over a gravel base being the favoured approach (Fig. 12). There is a tendency to use a shallower rootzone depth than for golf. From the point of view of the physics of soil water movement, this practice must be questioned and a deeper rootzone would be preferred. However bowls is primarily a summer sport and the shallower rootzone depth has usually been found to perform adequately in practice.

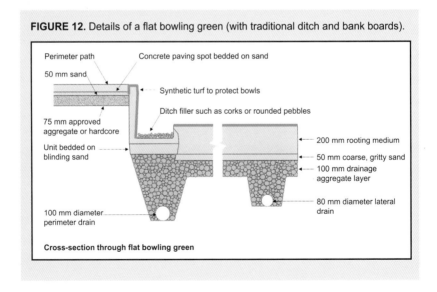

FIGURE 12. Details of a flat bowling green (with traditional ditch and bank boards).

Golf Bunkers

Green and fairway bunkers form a fundamental part of golf course design. On inland courses, bunkers should be constructed to give good drainage and certainly the ground contours should be shaped to avoid channelling surface run-off into the bunkers. Except in very free-draining subsoils, pipe drainage should be installed below the bunker floor. The drain trench is usually filled with gravel and covered with a suitable geotextile membrane which, on difficult gravelly or unstable soils, may also be used to cover the whole face of the bunker to prevent contamination of the sand. The sand itself will usually have a firmed depth of about 100 mm.

Revetted golf green bunker.

In selecting the sand, particularly for an inland course, there are a number of considerations:

(a)   The sand must be free-draining and not clog, causing water to pond at the surface. The size of the grains is also an important factor in the case of windblow and very fine materials should be avoided.

(b)   The sand may be chipped onto the green and therefore it should be compatible with top dressing material, i.e. free from coarse particles and of low lime content.

41

(c) The sand should be a fair hazard to the golfer and neither set as a crust (a characteristic of sands with a high fines content) nor allow the ball to plug excessively after a direct ball impact from a high iron shot. This can happen with coarse rounded sands and these can also be troublesome because of a lack of stable footing for the golfer.

(d) It is helpful if the sand is angular rather than rounded as this can increase the stacking angle at the bunker face.

(e) For golf bunkers, aesthetic conditions are also important and generally tan, light grey or white materials are preferred.

On links courses, drainage is generally satisfactory unless there are water table problems. Because fine dune sands are generally used in bunkers on seaside courses, it is wind erosion that is often the greatest problem. To minimise the effects of wind erosion, bunkers on links courses are usually relatively deep and narrow. Traditionally, the bunker face will have been stabilised by a wall of old fibrous turf sods laid to form a 'revetted' face of 1:1 or steeper.

Chapter 5
Soils for Cricket Pitches and Tennis Courts

Introduction

For most playing surfaces, imported materials are usually dominated by sand because of the need to sustain drainage, promote better aeration and to have a friable material that can be easily worked into the surface to restore levels and dilute any thatch build up. However, soils for cricket and tennis are very much the exception. For both these sports, there is a need to create a firm playing surface with good ball rebound properties. This is normally achieved using soils with a significant clay content which, on drying, helps bind the soil particles together.

Soils on Cricket Pitches

Construction profiles on cricket squares are very variable and, for example, at first-class level the depth of the clay loam layer varies from about 100 mm to 300 mm. Base construction varies from simple placement of the clay loam soil over the native soil to installation over a gravel base layer.

At club level soil depths are also variable. They can range from native soils with a heavier clay loam surface built up from repeated top dressing to excavated profiles where a clay loam soil has been installed. Normally, a minimum firmed depth of 100 mm is recommended for a good standard square used for club cricket.

A number of soil properties are important on cricket pitches: these include clay content, clay mineralogy, organic matter content, binding strength and shrinkage. These soil properties produce specific characteristics of pitches which are then modified during pitch preparation through compaction by rolling and control of soil moisture content through the use of pitch covers and the interaction with the rolling programme.

Clay content has a major effect on the binding properties of cricket soils and this affects the potential hardness of the surface. Clay contents of cricket soils vary widely in different parts of the world and according to the grade of cricket being played. Fig. 13 shows the distribution of clay content from pitches used for first-class cricket matches in the United Kingdom, with the majority of pitches having clay contents between 27-33%. In other parts of the world, clay contents are generally higher and Table 7 includes recent examples from other countries where cricket is played at first-class level. Climate conditions and, to an extent, clay mineralogy are important in influencing the type of soils used and, for example, drying rates are not high enough in the United Kingdom to justify the use of soils with clay contents higher than about 35%.

FIGURE 13. Distribution of clay content values for pitches used for first-class cricket in the United Kingdom (data from Baker *et al.* 1998).

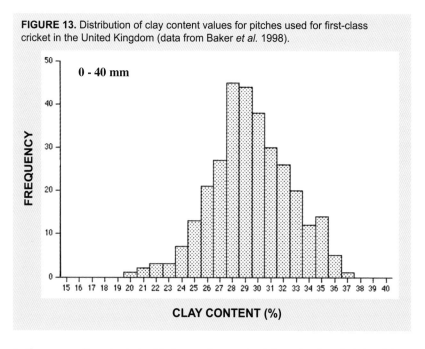

Soils are usually selected with lower clay content for school and club cricket. This normally reflects time and equipment available for pitch preparation, as heavier soils are more difficult to manage. For example, if pitch covers are not available, a heavier clay soil is hard to dry out. Reinstatement of grass cover may also be more difficult on some relatively infertile clay soils. However, cricket soils should normally have a clay content of at least 24% to ensure a reasonable degree of binding.

TABLE 7. Clay, silt and sand contents of soils used on cricket pitches in the United Kingdom, New Zealand and Australia.

	Clay	Silt	Sand	Soil types	Source
United Kingdom	23-35	42 (mean)	29 (mean)	Grounds used for first-day cricket	Baker *et al.* 1998a (0-40 mm depth)
New Zealand	46-69	25-47	6-20	Commonly used cricket soils	McAuliffe & Hannan 2001
Australia	51-82	6-22	6-32	Test match grounds	Lush *et al.* 1985

Clay mineralogy can have an influence on cricket soils. In the United Kingdom, the dominant clay minerals are kaolinite and illite, with some vermiculite and smectite. In New Zealand, the dominant clay minerals include vermiculite, kandite (kaolinite), smectite and mica. In Australia, montmorillonite clays are dominant with some illite and kaolinite.

Clay mineralogy influences hardness on drying, the degree of crumbling and shrinkage properties, for example shrinkage is likely to be greatest on smectitic clays. Organic matter content of cricket soils before grass establishment is usually in the range 3-8%. However, over time organic matter accumulates in the surface layer. In a typical profile of a first-class cricket pitch in the United Kingdom organic matter content would typically be 7-12% at 0-20 mm depth, 5-9 % at 20-40 mm depth and 4-7% at 60-80 mm depth.

Effect of Soil Properties on Cricket Pitch Performance

Clay content and organic matter content have a number of potential effects on pitch performance:

(a) The clay content of a soil affects its binding strength (Fig. 14) and in general as clay content increases the soil becomes harder, provided that drying rates are adequate.

(b) Increased organic matter reduces the bulk density (Fig. 15) that can be achieved and usually as organic matter increases the hardness of the surface and ball rebound both decrease. There is some evidence however that a moderate amount of organic matter at the surface (but not thatch) may either reduce friction or change the elasticity properties of the surface layer and increase the apparent pace of a pitch.

STRI trial on soil selection for cricket.

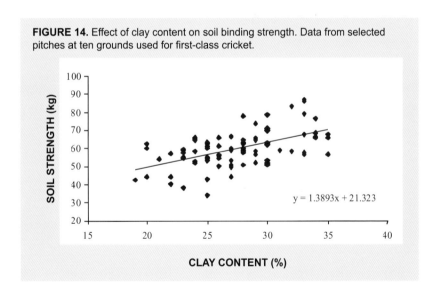

FIGURE 14. Effect of clay content on soil binding strength. Data from selected pitches at ten grounds used for first-class cricket.

$$y = 1.3893x + 21.323$$

(c) Greater clay content tends to increase soil shrinkage (Fig. 16) and the number of cracks and crack widths may be greater. Shrinkage and cracking patterns can also be influenced by organic matter content and clay mineralogy.

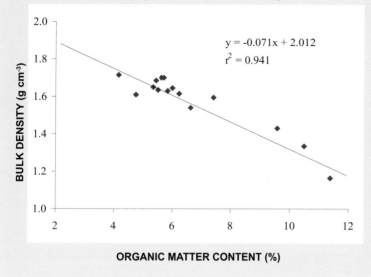

FIGURE 15. Effect of organic matter content on the bulk density of different cricket loams (0-20 mm depth) (data from Baker *et al.* 1998).

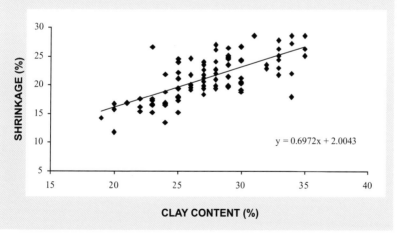

FIGURE 16. Effect of clay content on soil shrinkage. Data from selected pitches at ten grounds used for first-class cricket.

(d)	On a newly prepared pitch, there is little evidence to suggest that soil composition has a major effect on the spin of a ball. Spin appears to be influenced more by the preparation of a pitch in terms of moisture content and grass cover and by the amount of wear that occurs in the area where the ball lands. However, as a pitch becomes more worn, higher sand content and weaker binding strength may cause the soil to break up more easily. There is also some evidence that a higher sand content may increase friction between the ball and the surface, thus accentuating the effects of spin.

In reality the performance of different soils is the result of interaction between a range of soil characteristics and the way that the surface is managed and prepared for play. Fig. 17, for example, shows results for five selected soil characteristics associated with seven cricket loams used in the UK, managed as though for first-class cricket. The results are averaged over three assessment periods and show measured values on the first and fourth day of monitoring. The bulk density for most soils is around 1.75 g/cc but is notably lower on the two soils with higher organic matter contents. Similarly, moisture content is greater on the two soils with organic matter contents above 7%. Cracking patterns were very variable: crack length and width were least on the soil with only 24% clay. Crack lengths were generally greater on soils with higher organic matter contents while the soil based on a kaolinite clay was characterised by large, stable blocks with relatively wide cracks. Crack width increased considerably from the first to the fourth day of monitoring. Ball rebound was lowest on the two soils with high organic matter contents and greatest on the soil with the kaolinite clay. The soil with only 24% clay had notably high ball bounce values and this is attributed to a relatively low organic matter content and the influence that low clay content and organic matter content has on the rate of drying. Ball rebound height was consistently greater on the fourth day of monitoring.

Soils for Tennis Courts

Tennis courts are usually constructed using a layer of 75-100 mm of carefully selected loam soil which is spread over the existing topsoil following cultivation and grading. Any drainage is ideally installed around the perimeter of the court to avoid differential rates of drying and inconsistencies in performance.

FIGURE 17. Effect of soil type on the physical characteristics of cricket pitch (data from Baker *et al.* 2001, with data averaged over three monitoring periods). Light shading = day 1, dark shading = day 4.

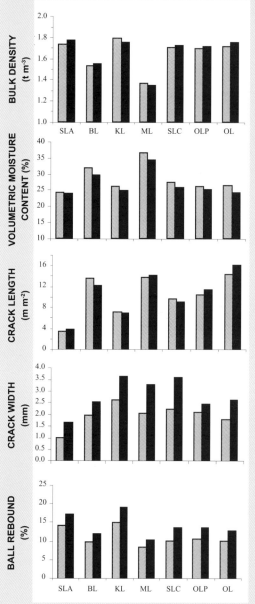

Soil code	Clay content (%)	Organic matter (%)
SLA	24	3.0
BL	30	7.1
KL	30	2.5
ML	30	7.8
SLC	31	2.8
OLP	31	3.8
OL	32	3.8

On sites with poor quality or impermeable subsoils, a 100 mm gravel carpet may be used for courts where the playing surface is to be constructed to a high standard. In this case, 200-250 mm of an imported topsoil would be used. The texture of the soil would generally be lighter than that used on a cricket pitch with, for example, 18-20% clay.

Grass tennis courts require sufficient clay in the soil for adequate binding.

Chapter 6

Top Dressing for Turf Management

Introduction

Top dressing practices vary considerably between sports, with very different materials being required for winter games pitches, golf and bowling greens, compared with cricket tables and tennis courts. Sand-dominated materials are required for most surfaces but clay rich soils are needed for cricket and tennis.

For winter games pitches, golf greens and bowling greens the properties of the turf vary according to the amount of play and level of compaction to which it is subjected. Increasing compaction will tend to reduce the permeability of the surface layer. This will be exacerbated if finer mineral particles migrate to the surface as a result of wear and if fine organic residues accumulate from the breakdown of grass material. On fine turf constructions, the accumulation of a thatchy, organic rich layer will have an important effect on the impact and roll of golf balls and the speed of bowls rolling across a green. Maintenance operations are essential to control the potential deterioration of turf resulting from compaction and organic matter production and sand-dominated top dressing has a vital function in any maintenance programme.

For cricket pitches and tennis courts, regular dressings of soil are important to reduce the build up of organic matter at the surface and to restore surface levels. However, soils must be selected so that they have the good binding properties that are important to allow the preparation of good, firm surfaces required for these two sports.

Winter Games Pitches

The main uses of sand in the maintenance programme for a winter games pitch is to dilute accumulations of fine mineral and organic matter at the surface to retain the permeability of a pitch and to provide a firmer surface in wet weather. In these circumstances, pure sand, with no soil amendment, is the preferred top dressing material. Sand or a sandy compost is also important to repair divots kicked out by the players, thus restoring the levels of the surface.

The advantages of sand are clearly seen in Fig. 18 which shows the effects of different rates of sand application on a pipe drained sandy loam soil, the same soil with slit drains at 600 mm centres and a sand carpet construction. The sand rates of 0, 4, 8 and 16 kg/m² per year correspond to annual applications

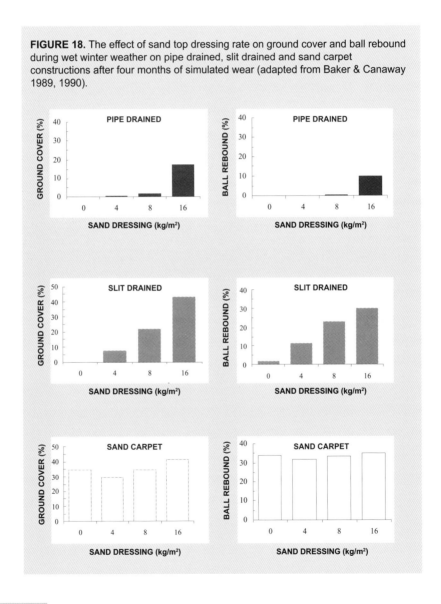

FIGURE 18. The effect of sand top dressing rate on ground cover and ball rebound during wet winter weather on pipe drained, slit drained and sand carpet constructions after four months of simulated wear (adapted from Baker & Canaway 1989, 1990).

of 0, 25, 50 and 100 tonnes of sand per year to a pitch of 6,250 m². The advantages of higher grades of construction were evident, with the sand carpet pitch retaining more cover during wear than the slit drained and particularly the pipe drained pitch. The sand carpet pitch also had a dry, firm surface where ball bounce, for example, was good. However, players find ball rebound values less than 15% unacceptable and the wet, muddy surface on some of the pipe drained and slit drained plots gave very low values indeed.

Sand application is important on all types of construction. Where topsoil is present, sand makes the surface layer less plastic in wet conditions and gives a firmer and drier surface. On sand constructions it can be important in maintaining surface permeability and diluting organic material which can accumulate in the areas of lower wear, e.g. on the wings. On a slit drained construction, the absence of protective sand dressings will invariably result in the slits being sealed by play, preventing rainfall from entering the slit system and causing waterlogged surfaces. In the example shown in Fig. 18, the grass cover on the sub-plots with no sand was zero compared with 43% cover where the equivalent of 100 tonnes of sand per year was used. The wet, muddy surface on the slit drained plots with no sand gave a ball rebound of only 1% compared with 30% on the area with the highest rate of sand.

The results for the slit drained plots with no sand are similar to those of the pipe drained area, in other words the advantages of a £30,000 slit drainage scheme can disappear in less than eighteen months of wear because of the lack of adequate sand dressing. Indeed, this trial and observations on actual pitches show that even a few months of play on a slit drained pitch with no sand dressing can negate the value of the drainage work.

Sand top dressing may also be used in conjunction with an aeration programme. For example, sand may be brushed into the surface following the use of a Verti-Drain or other form of deep aeration to stabilise the holes thus created.

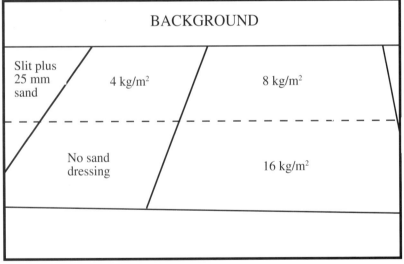

BACKGROUND

| Slit plus 25 mm sand | 4 kg/m² | 8 kg/m² |
| No sand dressing | | 16 kg/m² |

The effect of the rate of sand top dressing on grass retention at the end of a season of simulated wear on a slit drained construction. The treatment towards the rear on the left is a slit drained construction with a 25 mm sand top added at the construction stage.

Golf and Bowling Greens

On areas of fine turf, the main purpose of top dressing is to preserve a true and level surface and to dilute the build-up of thatch. Ideally, an annual application of 5-6 kg/m² of top dressing material should be used, with this quantity being divided into perhaps four to six applications to avoid excessive amounts of material on the surface at any one time. If the playing surface is on a heavy soil with poor drainage or has excess thatch, larger quantities should be applied following hollow tining so that the drainage and aeration of the upper part of the turf profile can be improved.

Top dressing application on a golf green.

The composition of the top dressing material may vary depending on the type of construction and the availability of topsoil materials or composts for the top dressing. Where a green has been constructed with a special rootzone mix, it is important to use a top dressing material which matches the mix in terms of the quantity of sand and the sand type. This will preserve continuity in the profile of the green.

Where a golf green has been developed from a native soil which may have a relatively high silt and clay content, it is sensible to use a relatively light top dressing material in which the clay content has been diluted by sand to below 3% and the total silt and clay content should not exceed 6%. The use of a sand which is dominated by the medium sand size fraction (0.25-0.5 mm diameter) is preferred for the preparation of this type of top dressing mix.

Sands with a high content of fine material should be avoided as these can clog the surface and excessively coarse sands create problems as it is difficult to work sand grains above 2 mm in diameter into the turf. Coarse particles such as these will damage mowers and are unpopular with golfers and bowlers.

Consistency in the use of top dressing materials on fine turf is important and, for instance, use of pure sand for perhaps a year followed by reversion to a sand-soil mix can form a root break. This thin layer of sand can have significant effects on the vertical movement of soil moisture and the penetration of grass roots will tend to reflect the moisture distribution within the soil.

In fine turf areas, the lime content of the top dressing material is critical. If the sand contains large quantities of shell or other calcareous material, the pH of the surface layer will increase. This can have important effects on weed invasion, earthworm activity, turfgrass disease and the composition of grass species within the turf. In particular, annual meadow-grass (*Poa annua*) will tend to invade the turf at the expense of the fescue (*Festuca*) and bent (*Agrostis*) species. With occasional exceptions (e.g. links courses), the lime content of any top dressing should be below 0.5% and preferably the material should be lime free.

Cricket Pitches and Tennis Courts

For cricket pitches, top dressing should be selected so that it is compatible with the soils on the pitch and helps maintain a surface that can be prepared to give a hard pitch with good pace and consistency of bounce. Compatibility is a vital issue with cricket pitch top dressings. Different soils have varying rates of drying and shrinkage, consequently when soils with different composition characteristics are added in layers this can lead to changes in physical properties and cracks between the layers. This tends to cause low and variable bounce. Problems can be accentuated if there are differences in fertility between the layers and root penetration is restricted or if layers of organic matter are sandwiched between the soil dressings.

Different soils have become fashionable over the years, or a new groundsman may have his own preferences, and some squares show the unfortunate legacy of these inconsistencies. Fortunately, the dangers of repeated changes of soil dressings has now been more widely recognised and management policies based on the use of a single good quality soil are now more widely adopted.

Development of layering within a cricket pitch profile because of changes in top dressing materials and bands of organic debris.

Top dressing on cricket pitches is usually carried out in the autumn at the end of the season, following scarification, renovation and aeration work. Normally, about 2-3 kg/m² is applied and top dressing should be applied over the whole of the square. Repeated dressings around the wicket ends causes an undesirable saddle profile to develop. Ground conditions and the clay loam top dressing must be dry to allow material to be spread and brushed into the surface properly. Similar principles are applicable for tennis courts with top dressing taking place at the end of the playing season as part of the renovation process. Application rates would typically be 2-3 kg/m² over the whole of the playing surface, as with cricket it is essential that the sward is thoroughly scarified to ensure that organic debris is not buried under the top dressing. Repeated dressings may sometimes be applied if levels are very poor or there is a need to replace an unsuitable surface soil with one of better quality. Lighter dressings of soil can sometimes be applied in the spring, for example at rates of 1-2 kg/m². Application should only be made if grass growth is good and the material can be quickly absorbed into the base of the sward before the start of the playing season.

Chapter 7

Guidelines for Sands for Sports Turf

Introduction

The objective of this section is to review the relevant literature on required sand types for specific applications for sports turf. This review and practical experience from laboratory testing and consultancy work then forms the basis of guidelines for sands for the varied applications on sports grounds, golf courses and bowling greens.

The guidelines for grain size and uniformity are given in the form of a grading envelope, i.e. a set of upper and lower size limits to which the sand should conform. This is considered to be more suitable for general application than, for instance, a system based on indices of grain size and uniformity. It is usually easier to plot the size distribution as a grading curve than to calculate the relevant size and uniformity indices and the latter are often difficult for users to comprehend.

The grading envelopes give a recommended and acceptable particle size distribution. If all the data points fit within the central band as in Sand A (Fig. 19), the sand would be considered to be in the recommended range for the specified application. If some of the points fall outside the central band, but within the overall grading envelope as in Sand B, the sand would be considered to be a potentially acceptable material but careful consideration of the particular conditions at the site would have to be made before its use could be confirmed. Sand B, for example, falls within the acceptable range but is slightly coarser than the preferred range. Obviously, if a sand was available which fell entirely into the central band (i.e. within the recommended limits), this should be chosen. To avoid any sands with a very wide size distribution being used for applications where there are likely to be high levels of compaction, a further stipulation is made. For rootzone and top dressing sands, if the sand is within the acceptable range but part of the distribution is coarser than the preferred limits and part finer than the preferred grading (e.g. Sand C), this material would not be acceptable. For Sand C, the D_{90}/D_{10} value is 8.7 which is clearly not acceptable. Finally, sands with any data point outside the acceptable grading envelope (e.g. Sand D) would not be considered acceptable.

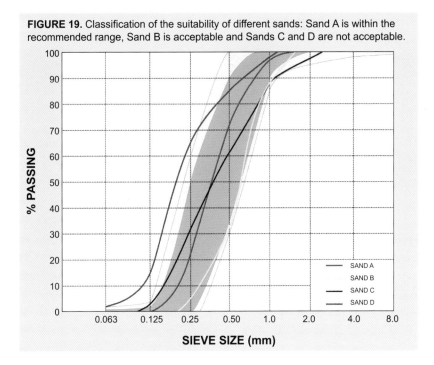

FIGURE 19. Classification of the suitability of different sands: Sand A is within the recommended range, Sand B is acceptable and Sands C and D are not acceptable.

Recommendations for lime content and particle shape are also given in association with each application for sports turf.

It is suggested that if the sand falls within the recommended range, this sand could be used with confidence for the intended application. If the sand falls within the acceptable range, it will be suitable in many cases although agronomic factors may preclude its use on certain sites or there may have to be slight modifications in, for example, a construction specification to accommodate the material. If there is any doubt about a sand's suitability, professional advice should be sought from a suitably qualified agronomist or soil scientist who can take into account the particular circumstances for which it is intended to use the sand.

In some cases, a sand may have been tested using a set of sieves of different mesh size to those used in this book. These laboratory results can be used but it must be remembered that a logarithmic scale is used on the horizontal size axis. The spacings on a logarithmic scale are not uniform and alternative sieve sizes are marked by a small tick at the top of each grading curve.

Winter Games Pitches

Recommendations for sands for winter games pitches have largely been based on research attempting to specify materials for the rootzone layer. In general, however, it is acceptable to use these criteria in specifying sand for top dressing as well. Comparison of published recommendations is complicated by the fact that some specifications are based on the final composition of the rootzone layer and others are simply recommendations for the sand component of the rootzone mix or for a pure sand construction. A summary of existing recommendations is given in Table 8 and where possible the exact application is stated.

Guidelines for sands for winter games pitches

Grading   : sand component for use in rootzone mixes and top dressing
               (see Fig. 20)
Lime content : <1%.
Particle shape : not specified, although sub-rounded to sub-angular materials
               are preferred

Normally, the aim would be to obtain a sand falling within the darker central area of the grading curve. There are two main exceptions:

i)   If only relatively light applications of sand are used (<25 tonnes per pitch per year) it is generally more effective to use a sand within the coarser range of the recommended limits.

ii)   In rare situations where pure sand rootzones are used it would be sensible to avoid materials coarser than the preferred range otherwise there could be significant problems with water retention and surface stability.

TABLE 8. Published recommendations for sands for winter games pitches.

Authors	Application	Size range (mm)	Other criteria
Dutch Working Group (1970)	Specification for rootzone	0.1-0.5	Require that the D_{50} value is between 0.13-0.23 mm and that no more than 10% of the particles are <20 µm.
Adams et al. (1971)	Rootzone sand	0.1-0.6	Ideally the sand would have a D_{90}/D_{10} of approximately 2.5 with both the D_{90} and D_{10} values in the range 0.1-0.6 mm
Bingaman & Kohnke (1970)	Rootzone sand	0.1-0.5	D_{50} between 0.2-0.4 mm. Clay, silt and very fine sand essentially absent. D_{95}/D_5 between 2-6.
Harper (undated)	Sand for soil modification	0.25-2.0	Paper suggests that "at least 80% of the sand be between 2.0 and 0.5 or 1.0 and 0.25 mm. Narrower size ranges would be desirable".
Harper (undated)	Pure sand rootzone	0.125-2.0	Recommends sands having 60% in the range 0.25-0.5 mm and 95% in the range 0.125-2.0 mm.
Mulqueen (1983)	Rootzone sand	0.1-2.5	Specification is presented as a grading curve. Sizes are the D_{10} and D_{90} values taken from the centre of the grading limits.
Baker (1983, 1984)	Rootzone sand	0.125-0.5	It is noted that a slightly higher proportion of very fine sand can be tolerated in an all-sand construction than when the sand is used for soil amelioration.
Skirde (1989)	Specification for rootzone	0.06-2.0	Specification is presented as a grading curve. Sizes are the D_{10} and D_{90} values taken from the centre of the grading limits.
Baker (1990)	Rootzone and top dressing sand	0.15-0.75	Specification is presented as a grading curve. Values given are the minimum D_{10} and maximum D_{90} values from the preferred range.
Stewart (1994)	Rootzone sand	0.125-0.75	Specification is presented as grading limits. Sizes are the D_{10} and D_{90} values taken from the centre of the grading limits.
Sports Turf Association (1991)	Sand suitable for sportsfield construction	0.1-0.6	80% in 0.1-0.6 mm range. Mid-particle diameter between 0.15-0.25 mm. No more than 3% <0.1 mm and no more than 3% >1.0 mm.

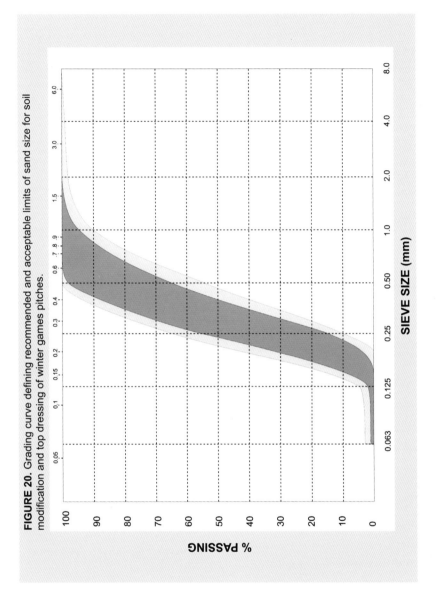

FIGURE 20. Grading curve defining recommended and acceptable limits of sand size for soil modification and top dressing of winter games pitches.

Golf and Bowling Greens

Existing recommendations of sand for fine turf are given in Table 9. Some earlier recommendations for sand-soil mixes favoured relatively coarse materials but over the past thirty years the general consensus has been to use high sand contents with uniform medium or medium-coarse materials.

TABLE 9. Existing recommendations for sands for golf and bowling greens.

Authors	Application	Size range (mm)	Other criteria
Daniel (1972)	Rootzone sand	0.25-0.5	Uniformity is emphasised. The material should be free from clay, fine silt and coarse gravel.
Davis (1973)	Rootzone sand	0.1-1.0	Suggests 85-95% in range 0.1-1.0 mm with over 60% between 0.25-0.5 mm. No more than 10% >1.0 mm with no particles >2.38 mm.
Radko (1974)	Sand for soil mixtures	0.15-1.0	Exact specification for the ideal sand is 100% <1.0 mm, 35% <0.5 mm, 15% <0.25 mm 5% <0.06 mm. Detailed specifications are also made for the final rootzone mixture.
Waddington (1976)	Sand for soil mixes	Either 0.5-2.0 0.25-1.0	Suggest at least 80% of the sand in either category. A narrower specification would be preferred but this has implications on availability and costs.
Waddington (1976)	Rootzone sand	0.1-0.5	At least 85% centred in 0.1-0.5 mm range.
Murphy & Nelson (1979)	Rootzone sand		No more than 20% of particles <0.5 mm.
Blake (1980)	Sand for soil mixes	0.25-1.0	Exact specification is: Fineness modulus[†] 1.7-2.5, D_{60}/D_{10} <4. Particles <0.1 mm <3%. Particles >2.0 mm <3%. Particles 0.25-1.0 mm >60%.
Baker (1984)	Sand for soil mixes	0.2-0.7	Distribution centred on range 0.25-0.5 mm.
Baker (1990)	Rootzone sand	0.15-1.0	Specification is presented as a grading curve. Values given are the minimum D_{10} and maximum D_{90} values from the preferred range.
USGA Green Section Staff (2004)	Sand for soil mixes	0.25-1.0	"Fine sands [0.25 to 0.10 mm] and particularly very fine sands [0.10 to 0.05 mm] should be kept to minimum levels and, when present at all, should comprise no more than 10% of the total mix."

[†] Fineness modulus is the sum of the cumulative percentages retained on the 4.76, 2.38, 1.19, 0.595, 0.297 and 0.149 mm sieves divided by 100.

The guideline which is given is based on a sand material for sand-dominated mixes in which the final sand content is to be >90%. The Sports Turf Research Institute does not recommend pure sand constructions for fine turf so a specification for sands for this application is not given. On links courses, it is better to match any imported sand with the natural fine to medium dune sands on which links courses are based and under these circumstances the grading curve for winter games pitches (Fig. 20) is more appropriate.

Lime content presents less of a problem on links courses. In such areas, exposure to wind and salt spray and the very sandy substrate mean that the grasses are less affected by calcareous conditions. Accordingly, the normal recommendations of lime-free sands can often be relaxed.

The guideline which is given is appropriate for sands for both construction and top dressing.

Guidelines for sands for golf and bowling greens

Grading   : see Fig. 21
Lime content : <0.5% but preferably lime-free
Particle shape : not specified, although rounded to sub-angular materials are
                preferred.

If dressings of pure sand are made to improve the drainage and firmness of golf fairways, it would be more appropriate to use the grading curve for winter games pitches given in Fig. 20. Normally, lime-free sand should be used.

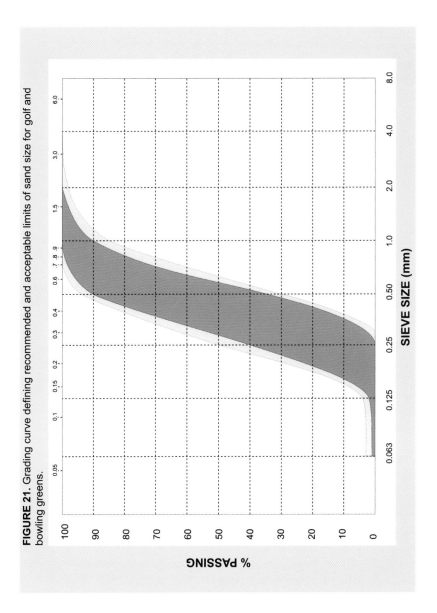

FIGURE 21. Grading curve defining recommended and acceptable limits of sand size for golf and bowling greens.

Blinding Sands

The function of the blinding layer is to prevent soil over drain trenches from contaminating the gravel backfill in the trench or, in the case of a construction with a gravel drainage carpet, the blinding sand prevents the finer root-zone material from migrating downwards into the gravel.

In theory, for materials with a uniform size distribution, a sand will not migrate downwards if its diameter is greater than one sixth of the diameter of the underlying layer. Where the respective materials have a slightly wider size distribution, and therefore some interlocking of particles, this figure can be relaxed slightly and the following relationship is now widely accepted as a suitable bridging factor:–

D_{15} (gravel) should be less than or equal to 8 x D_{85} (rootzone) where:

D_{15} (gravel)   =   Diameter with 15% by mass passing for the gravel
D_{85} (rootzone)   =   Diameter with 85% by mass passing for the rootzone

For a layered construction where rootzone sand is placed over gravel, it follows that the blinding layer must be compatible with the gravel but also that the rootzone sand must not migrate into the blinding sand. It should be noted, however, when soil is added over a drain trench, aggregation of the soil particles is usually sufficient to prevent migration of particles into the blinding layer overlying the gravel backfill of the trench.

Existing recommendations for blinding sands (Table 10) are complicated by the fact that the size of the gravel does vary depending on the availability of local materials. These guidelines vary from the use of a relatively uniform, coarse sand, in the case of the USGA recommendation, to sands with a wider spread of material for which interlocking of particles is important in preventing downwards migration of the finer fraction. In Britain, there are no natural sands with a uniform 1-2 mm size distribution and hence sands with a wider spread of particles were generally used for blinding purposes. However, with better processing, a range of 1-4 mm grits are now available.

The guidelines for blinding sands cannot be considered in isolation from the size distribution of the gravel material which requires blinding. In general, gravel materials in the range 5-10 mm are used in sports turf drainage and the guideline which is given is based on a gravel falling within this range with a mid-particle diameter (D_{50}) of no more than 8 mm. For a coarse gravel with a D_{50} value in the range 8-10 mm, the points on the grading curve should fall within a zone coarser than the finer recommended limit. Similarly, if the root-zone sand is relatively fine (i.e. with a D_{50} value <0.25 mm), the blinding sand should be finer than the upper recommended limit with no points in the coarse but acceptable zone.

TABLE 10. Published recommendations for blinding sands.

Authors	Application	Size range (mm)	Other criteria
Radko (1974)	Blinding of 6.4 mm per gravel	>1.0	
Adams (1982)	Blinding over 6 mm gravel	>0.2	To prevent infiltering at least 20% >1.0. A wide range in particle size is useful.
Baker (1984)		0.3-2.0	1.0-2.0 as dominant size range.
Baker (1990)	Blinding of a 5-10 mm gravel	0.25-3.0	Specification is presented as a grading curve. Values given are the minimum D_{10} and maximum D_{90} values from the preferred range.
Stewart (1994)	Blinding of 3-10 mm gravel having 82-100% passing 10 mm and 0-6% passing 2.0 mm	0.15-3.5	Specification is presented as grading limits. Sizes are the D_{10} and D_{90} values taken from the centre of the grading limits.
Baker & Binns (2001)	Blinding of a predominantly 6-9 mm gravel	0.5-4.0	Values given are based on the D_{10} and D_{90} value of a proposed grading.
USGA Green Section Staff (2004)	Blinding of predominantly 6-9 mm gravel	1.0-4.0	90% in 1.0-4.0 mm size range.

Guidelines for blinding sands over a 5-10 mm drainage aggregate

Grading   : see Fig. 22
Lime content : <15%. Furthermore, soft limestone fragments must be avoided
Particle shape : not specified

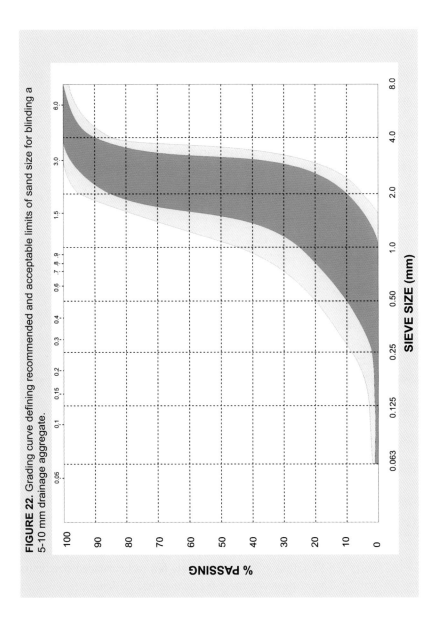

FIGURE 22. Grading curve defining recommended and acceptable limits of sand size for blinding a 5-10 mm drainage aggregate.

Slit Drainage Sands

Sands for slit drainage must fulfil a number of requirements. They should be of high permeability to allow the rapid transfer of water to the drains, but at the same time be sufficiently water-retentive to support grass growth. Furthermore, sands should be sufficiently stable so that if grass cover is lost on a winter games pitch the sand will not kick out of the slits nor detract from the playing quality of the surface. Coarse particles in the sand should not affect the quality of the surface and, finally, if the slit is a layered construction of the sand over more permeable gravel, then the sand must not migrate downwards into the gravel.

Where slits are installed without a lower layer of gravel (e.g. secondary slit systems based on sand banding or surface grooving) it is possible to use a relatively uniform medium sand. The grading for sands for fine turf (Fig. 21) is an appropriate guideline for the sand selection.

However, in many slit drainage designs the slits consist of sand over gravel. An example could be 100 mm of sand over 125 mm gravel depending on the slit and drain spacings and the target drainage design rates. The gravel is preferred because of its capacity to transmit water laterally to the drains, for example a slit drain of 100 mm sand over 125 mm of 5-8 mm gravel would have a lateral drainage capacity over five times that of a slit of 225 mm medium sand.

If very coarse gravels are used in the slit drains, the sand would also need to be relatively coarse to satisfy the blinding criteria. The sands may be rather unstable and abrasive to players and re-establishment of grass over the slits could be difficult. It helps, therefore, if slightly finer gravels of approximately 5-8 mm are used in the slit drains and it is for this type of material that the specification is derived.

In the sports turf literature, there are relatively few recommended size limits for slit drainage sands. However, these are summarised in Table 11.

TABLE 11. Published recommendations for sands for slit drainage.

Authors	Application	Size range (mm)	Other criteria
Stewart (1972)	Sand slits (no gravel)		Clean, fine sand with uniform particle size, like dune sand.
Stewart (1973)	Sand/gravel slits	0.2-2.0	
Adams (1986)	Sand/gravel slits		Zone 2 concreting sand.
Baker (1984)	[i] Sand slits	0.25-1.0	
	[ii] Sand/gravel slits	0.3-2.0	
Baker (1990)	[i] Sand slits	0.2-1.5	Specification is presented as a grading curve. Values given are the minimum D_{10} and maximum D_{90} values from the preferred range.
	[ii] Sand/gravel slits	0.2-2.5	

Guidelines for slit drainage sands for placement
over a 5-8 mm gravel in the base of the slit

Grading   : see Fig. 23
Lime content : [i] for most winter games pitches <1%
                        [ii] for golf fairways, hockey pitches or cricket outfields where
                               fine turf grass species are present <0.5%
Particle shape : not specified

Golf Bunkers

Published recommendations for bunker sands are given in Table 12 and in general reflect a compromise between the requirements of playing quality, drainage, stability and resistance to windblow.

In determining the best sands for golf bunkers, the characteristics of the course must be considered as there is a difference in the requirements for inland courses and seaside links. The grading curves which are given are primarily designed for inland courses although the finer acceptable limit would encompass sands on many links courses. There are some links courses with yet finer sand particles, e.g. concentrated around 0.15 mm. Where such sands are the natural material on the course, forming the growing medium for the greens and fairways, it is obviously sensible to use this type of sand. The fact that most bunkers on links courses are deeper and often smaller than their counterparts on inland courses also helps reduce the danger of windblow. In a similar

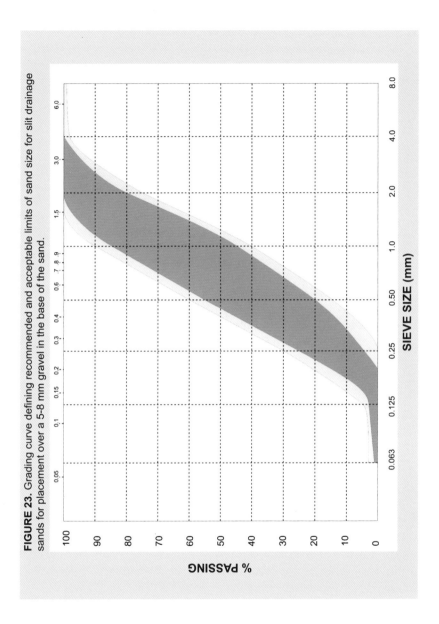

FIGURE 23. Grading curve defining recommended and acceptable limits of sand size for slit drainage sands for placement over a 5-8 mm gravel in the base of the sand.

71

TABLE 12. Existing recommendations for bunker sands.

Authors	Application	Size range (mm)	Other criteria
USGA Green Section Staff (1974)		0.25-1.0	Ideally 75% between 0.25-0.5 mm.
O'Brien (1985)		0.25-1.0	Ideally 75% between 0.25-0.5 mm.
Brown & Thomas (1986)		0.1-1.0	At least 78% between 0.1-1.0 mm. No more than 15% >1.0 mm. Criteria also given for ball penetration and other physical properties.
Baker et al. (1990)	[i] Inland courses [ii] Links courses	0.25-1.0 0.125-0.5	
Baker (1990)	Inland courses	0.2-1.0	Specification is presented as a grading curve. Values given are the minimum D_{10} and maximum D_{90} values from the preferred range.
Dixon (1992)		Mainly 0.25-1.0	75% 0.25-0.5 mm but up to 17% 0.05-0.25 permissible.
Australian Golf Union/ATRI (1995)	[i] Inland courses [ii] Links courses	0.2-1.0 0.1-1.0	Criteria also given for angularity, shape, angle of repose and other physical properties.

manner, lime content through shell material on a links course does not present the problems which would occur inland. If the golf course is relatively exposed and windblow is likely to be a problem, the sand which is used should not be finer than the finer recommended limit.

Guidelines for bunker sands on inland courses

Grading : see Fig. 24
Lime content : <0.5% but preferably lime-free
Particle shape : no more than 60% of particles in the rounded and well-rounded shape categories (see Fig. 3)
Colour : white, tan or light grey preferred

Consideration should also be given to the uniformity of the sand size distribution. Very uniform sands, particularly those with rounded grains, may be fluffy and prone to instability. Sands with a D_{90}/D_{10} gradation index of 2.5 or more are preferable.

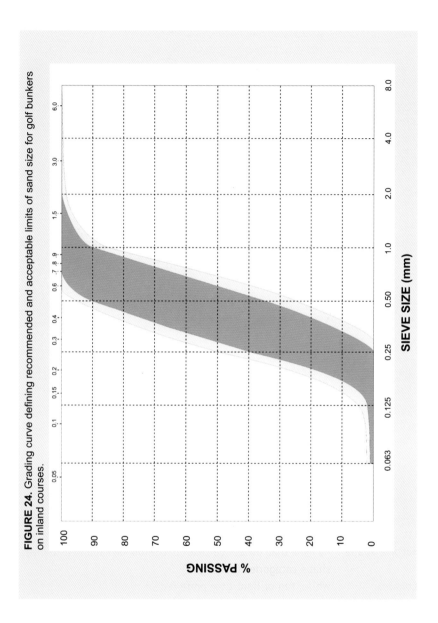

FIGURE 24. Grading curve defining recommended and acceptable limits of sand size for golf bunkers on inland courses.

Chapter 8
Guidelines for Rootzones and Top Dressing

Introduction

In this chapter, the selection of rootzone and top dressing materials is considered for a range of sports. Preferred materials can vary from rootzone blends with a high sand content for golf greens and winter games pitches to clay loam soils for cricket pitches.

In most cases, the top dressing should match the rootzone material, as compatibility between successive layers is important. The main exception is winter games pitches. Grass on football and Rugby pitches is either grown on the native soil or on a sandy rootzone containing a soil amendment but top dressing is normally based on pure sand.

The information presented primarily addresses the physical properties, lime content and pH of rootzones and top dressings. Two other factors however also need to be taken into account:

(a) The material should not be toxic and contaminants harmful to plant growth (e.g. heavy metals or other pollutants) should be absent. If there are doubts, a growth test (e.g. using mustard seed) or chemical testing should be carried out.
(b) The material should generally be free from weed material or the seeds of weedgrass species. The degree of sterility required may vary depending on the application. Complete sterilisation through heating or chemical means does have implications for cost.

Golf Greens

There are a number of possible methods to construct high quality golf greens, but all include sand as the basic main component of the rootzone mix. For convenience, two groups of construction methods may be recognised:

(a) Constructions with a gravel drainage layer. This method is most suitable for sites with poor draining native soils.

(b) Constructions where the sand-dominated rootzone is placed on either the existing sandy and free-draining soil of the site or a layer of sand is laid before installation of the rootzone material.

In most cases, a pipe drainage system will be installed at the base of the green, but on some sites with very permeable underlying soils (e.g. links or heathland courses) this may not always be needed.

Where rootzone mixes overlie a gravel drainage layer, the most widely used guidelines are those given by the USGA. These have been updated a number of times over the years and a summary of the current guidelines is given in Tables 13 and 14.

The USGA guidelines cover a very wide range of potential climatic conditions ranging from desert and sub-tropical environments to more temperate latitudes. For the more restricted climatic temperate, maritime conditions found in the United Kingdom, more specific guidelines have been published by the STRI in 2005. These have been developed primarily for courses based on less permeable soils for which good drainage and the inclusion of a gravel base layer is essential to give good year round playing performance. Particle size requirements for the rootzone mix are given in Fig. 25 and requirements for physical properties on compacted rootzone mixes are given in Table 15.

Where mixes are prepared to be placed on a base of fine sand or free-draining natural soils, the rootzone mix is often finer than when a gravel layer is included. Various requirements from published literature are given in Table 16.

No specific guidelines are given for situations where golf green rootzones are placed directly over existing sandy soils, e.g. for links or heathland courses. Detailed information on the site conditions and design requirements is needed. Normally, a golf course architect or agronomist would have to make recommendations for the rootzone based on a detailed assessment of site conditions.

TABLE 13. Particle size distribution of USGA rootzone mix (USGA Green Section Staff 2004).

Name	Particle diameter (mm)	Recommendation (by weight)
Fine gravel Very coarse sand	2.0-3.4 } 1.0-2.0	Not more than 10% of the total particles, including a maximum of 3% fine gravel (preferably none)
Coarse sand Medium sand	0.5-1.0 } 0.25-0.50	Minimum of 60% of the particles must fall in this range
Fine sand	0.15-0.25 }	Not more than 20% of the particles may fall within this range
Very fine sand Silt Clay	0.05-0.15 } 0.002-0.05 <0.002	Not more than 5% } Total particles in Not more than 5% } this range shall not Not more than 3% } exceed 10%

TABLE 14. Physical properties of the rootzone mix for a USGA green (USGA Green Section Staff 2004).

Physical property	Recommended range
Total porosity	35-55%
Air-filled porosity (at 30 cm tension)	15-30%
Capillary porosity (at 30 cm tension)	15-25%
Saturated conductivity	Minimum of 150 mm/hr

FIGURE 25. Grading curve for rootzones for golf courses in the United Kingdom.

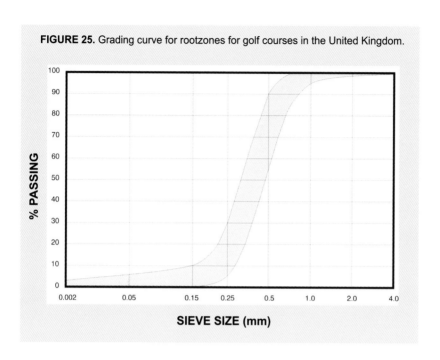

SIEVE SIZE (mm)

TABLE 15. Physical and chemical properties for the rootzone mix for golf greens (STRI 2005).

Parameter	Requirement
Total porosity	>35%
Air-filled porosity (30 cm tension)	>14%
Capillary porosity (30 cm tension)	>17%
Hydraulic conductivity	>150 mm/hr
Organic matter content	0.5-3.5%
Lime content	<0.5%
pH	5.5-7.0

TABLE 16. Recommendations for golf green rootzones placed over a sandy base or sandy-textured soil.

Author	Context	Recommendations
Davis (1973)	Fine sand greens	85-95% 0.1-1.0 mm, 2-8% <0.1 mm.
Baker (2003)	Dutch golf greens	Particle size predominantly 0.15-0.5 mm. 75-95% passing 0.5 mm, 6-15% passing 0.15 mm and 2-5% silt plus clay.

Bowling Greens

For the production of free-draining high quality rootzones, the guidelines for golf given in Fig. 25 and Table 15 would be appropriate. Bowls is however played primarily in the spring, summer and early autumn and therefore less permeable mixes with higher contents of silt and clay are often used. Table 17 summarises criteria outlined by Evans (1992) for the preparation of the rootzone mixes which are free-draining yet contain sufficient clay fraction to sustain reasonably healthy growth and prevent over-susceptibility to drought.

TABLE 17. Criteria for preparation of rootzone mixes for bowls (from Evans 1992).

Clay content (<0.002 mm)	No more than 5%
Clay, silt and very fine sand (<0.125 mm)	No more than 20%
Sand (0.05-2.0 mm)	At least 80%. Majority in the medium to medium-coarse range (0.25-1.0 mm)

Laboratory testing of soil physical properties (e.g. hydraulic conductivity and air-filled porosity) is needed to confirm the suitability of the rootzone material.

Winter Games Pitches

Details of existing recommendations for the sand component of winter games pitches have already been outlined (Table 8). In the UK, there are no formal guidelines for rootzone mixes for winter games pitches. However, Fig. 26 includes examples of rootzone mixes used at six professional soccer grounds, all of which performed well and were considered to be in the top three pitches in the Premier League and Football League Championship in an awards scheme in 2004.

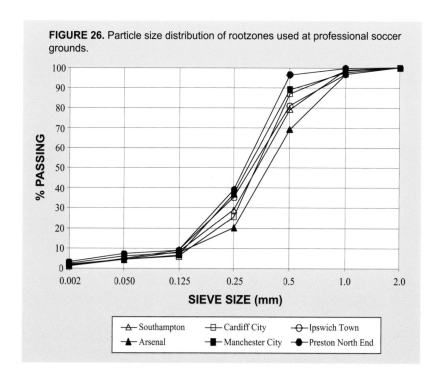

FIGURE 26. Particle size distribution of rootzones used at professional soccer grounds.

Legend:
- —△— Southampton
- —□— Cardiff City
- —⊖— Ipswich Town
- —▲— Arsenal
- —■— Manchester City
- —●— Preston North End

X-axis: SIEVE SIZE (mm) — 0.002, 0.050, 0.125, 0.25, 0.5, 1.0, 2.0

Y-axis: % PASSING — 0 to 100

Cricket Pitches

Guidelines for soils for cricket pitches vary depending on the standard of play and from country to country, because of the influence of climatic conditions and the grass types that are used. Published requirements given in Table 18 relate exclusively to soils for pitches in the United Kingdom. They would also apply to other moist temperate climate zones. Heavier soils are normally preferred in other parts of the world that have higher rates of evapotranspiration and therefore greater capability of drying the soil to optimum values.

Two sets of guidelines are given in this book: one for use for first-class cricket and high quality club standard, the other for general club standard and school cricket (Table 19). The choice of the appropriate guidelines will be dictated primarily by the standard of the playing surface that is required and the resources available (e.g. heavy rollers and covers) for pitch preparation and management.

TABLE 18. Existing recommendations for soils for cricket pitches in the United Kingdom.

Author	Context	Recommendations
Stewart & Adams (1968)	County cricket	Clay 25-40%.
STRI (1980)	Top dressing, club squares	Clay 25-30%, free from grit.
Adams (1983)	Top dressing for club cricket	Clay 24-30%. Silt/(sand + silt) not more than 0.75. Stones (>2 mm) less than 1%. Binding strength not less than 40 kg. Organic matter 4-15%. pH not below 5.5.
Adams (1983)	Top dressing for county cricket	Clay 28-38%. Silt/(sand + silt) not more than 0.75. Stones (>2 mm) less than 1%. Binding strength no less than 55 kg. Organic matter 4-15%. pH not below 5.5.
ECB (2000)	First-class and premier leagues	Clay 28-35%. Binding strength 65-90 kg. Organic matter 2-8%.
	Club standard	Clay 25-30%. Binding strength 55-65 kg. Organic matter 2-8%.
	School	Clay 25-28%. Organic matter 2-8%.
Adams et al. (2004)	First-class standard	Clay 27-33%. Organic matter 3-8%.

TABLE 19. Recommendations for the selection of cricket soils.

First-class cricket and high quality club standard	Clay content	27-33%
	Silt content	Not more than 50%
	Particles >2 mm	Not more than 1%
	Organic matter content	3-8%
	Binding strength	Not less than 55 kg
	pH	Not less than 5.5
General club standard/ schools	Clay content	24-32%
	Silt content	Not more than 60%
	Particles >2 mm	Not more than 2%
	Organic matter content	3-8%
	Binding strength	Not less than 40 kg
	pH	Not less than 5.5

Tennis Courts

Few recommendations have been published concerning soil selection for grass tennis courts (Table 20). More detailed guidelines for soils for tennis courts are given in Table 21.

TABLE 20. Existing recommendations for soils for grass tennis courts.

Author	Context	Recommendations
Pool (2000)	Construction material	Clay content 18-20%.
McClements (2000)	Top dressing	Clay content 15-20%. Stone content (particles greater than 2 mm) <1%. Binding strength >35 kg.

TABLE 21. Guidelines for soils for tennis courts.

Clay content	15-22*
Silt content	<55
Coarse particles above 2 mm	<1
Binding strength (kg)	>35
Organic matter content (%)	4-10
pH	>5.5

* Clay contents above 20% are only appropriate for courts where intensive maintenance can be applied and high standards are required.

Chapter 9

Supply, Testing and Ordering of Construction and Top Dressing Materials

Quality Control

Soils and sands are natural materials and never totally uniform in terms of their texture, grain size or chemical properties. Soils can vary depending from which part of a field they are taken and for sand the variability of particle size in a deposit is a function of the agents of transportation and settlement at the time when the sand was deposited. Similarly, processing of sands can vary. Sands developed for certain industrial applications, e.g. glassmaking, filter beds, etc. should be consistent because they are processed to satisfy the grading requirements of these industries. However, many of the building sands have less stringent requirements and variations in the degree of washing can affect the quality of the sand.

Preparation of a rootzone at mixing plant.

It is important, therefore, to recognise the fact that although soils, sands and rootzones may initially satisfy gradings given in this book, further supplies of material from a different part of a field or quarry may not meet the same grading curves. Regular testing is required as part of the quality control programme for materials supply, particularly if there are doubts whether material still meets a given requirement.

Testing should be carried out by a specialised laboratory where it should be possible to identify the most appropriate tests for sports turf applications. For the testing of materials for top dressing and rootzone mixes, the laboratory should have A2LA accreditation and the STRI laboratories are one of only two laboratories in Europe to have this accreditation (Appendix I).

Many of the more reputable suppliers of sands, rootzones and top dressing material have high standards of quality control with regular testing of their products. Testing work may be carried out within a company's own laboratories but, for example, members of the British Rootzone and Top dressing Manufacturers' Association (BRTMA) also send materials to the STRI laboratories for analysis.

Ordering Construction and Top Dressing Materials

Conversion of volumetric to weight requirements

Many of the estimates of sand and rootzone requirements are based on volumetric quantities rather than weight. It is usually then necessary to convert the volumetric requirement to a weight basis for the purpose of ordering, making due allowance for the effects of consolidation. One cubic metre of damp, loose sand can weigh as little as 1.3 tonnes after drying but, more typically, the bulk density of sand (i.e. the dry weight per unit volume) is 1.6 tonnes/m^3. Moisture content of sand usually varies from around 2-6% (except for sands dried during processing) and there are also potential losses, particularly if the sand is stockpiled over native soil or turf at a site and cannot all be recovered without contamination. It is therefore usually best to assume that 1.65 to 1.7 tonnes of sand are required for each cubic metre of firmed sand material.

For sand-dominated rootzones or top dressing, the conversion factor is influenced by the type of mixture. A blend of sand and peat or sand with another organic matter source would have a conversion factor of around 1.6-1.65 t/m^3, while for a sand/soil mix, a density of 1.65-1.70 t/m^3 would be more appropriate.

For clay-rich soils for cricket pitches and tennis courts, a conversion factor of 1.6 t/m^3 is usually an appropriate guideline.

Checking of delivered materials

The quality of some sands does vary depending on which part of a pit it is extracted from and the degree of processing. Similarly, the quality of soils can vary depending on the source. Ideally, a sample of the approved sand or soil should be retained or a required grading envelope should be specified and each load which is delivered should be compared with this material.

If there appears to be a departure from the approved material, laboratory testing may be required. All delivery notes should be retained to ensure that the correct total is delivered on site.

References and Selected Bibliography

Rootzones, sands and top dressing: general

Adams, W.A. (1976). The effect of fine soil fractions on the hydraulic conductivity of sand/soil mixes used for sports turf rootzones. *Razen Turf Gazon* **4**, 92-94.

Adams, W.A. (1981). Soils and plant nutrition for sports turf : perspective and prospects. In: *Proc. 4th Int. Turfgrass Conf.*, Guelph, Canada, (Ed. R.W. Sheard), July, pp. 167-179.

Adams, W.A. & Butters, H. (1997). Root-zone formulation, anomalous behaviour and testing of physical properties. *Int. Turfgrass Soc. Res. J.* **8**, 27-36.

Adams, W.A. & Gibbs, R.J. (1994). *Natural Turf for Sports and Amenity: Science and Practice*. CAB International, Cambridge, 404 pp.

Adams, W.A. & Jones, R.L. (1979). The effect of particle size composition and root binding on the resistance to shear of sports turf surfaces. *Rasen Grunflachen Begrunungen* **10** (2), 48-53.

Baker, S.W. (1983). Sands for soil amelioration: analysis of the effects of particle size, sorting and shape. *J. Sports Turf Res. Inst.* **59**, 133-145.

Baker, S.W. (1984). Long-term effects of three amendment materials on the moisture retention characteristics of a sand-soil mix. *J. Sports Turf Res. Inst.* **60**, 61-65.

Baker, S.W. (1984). Choosing the exact sand required for the job. *Parks, Golf Courses & Sports Grounds* **49** (12), 30-34.

Baker, S.W. (1985). Topsoil quality: relation to the performance of sand-soil mixes. In: *Proc. 5th Int. Turfgrass Res. Conf.*, Avignon, France (Ed. F. Lemaire), pp. 401-409.

Baker, S.W. (1990). *Sands for Sports Turf Construction and Maintenance*. Sports Turf Research Institute, Bingley, 71 pp.

Baker, S.W. & Binns, D.J. (2001). The influence of grain size and shape on particle migration from the rootzone layer to the drainage layer of golf greens. *Int. Turfgrass Soc. Res. J.* **9**, 458-462.

Baker, S.W., Gibbs, R.J. & Taylor, R.S. (1991). Particle migration from the sand layer of slit drains into the underlying gravel. *J. Sports Turf Res. Inst.* **67**, 93-104.

Bauer, H.P., Beckett, P.H.T. & Bie, S.W. (1972). A rapid gravimetric method for estimating calcium carbonate in soils. *Plant & Soil* **37**, 689-690.

Bigelow, C.A., Bowman, D. & Cassel, K. (2000). Sand-based rootzone modification with inorganic soil amendments and sphagnum peat moss. *USGA Green Section Record*, July/August, pp. 7-13.

Bingaman, D.E. & Kohnke, H. (1970). Evaluating sands for athletic turf. *Agron. J.* **62**, 464-467.

Blake, G.R. (1980). Proposed standards and specifications for quality of sands for soil-sand-peat mixes. In: *Proc. 3rd Int. Turfgrass Res. Conf.*, Munich, Germany (Ed. J.B. Beard), pp. 195-203.

BS 410:2000. *Test Sieves*. British Standards Institution, 18 pp.

Daniel, W.H. (1970). Ten ways to construct rootzones for turf areas. *Rasen Turf Gazon* **2** (70), 106-107.

Daniells, I.G. (1977). Drainage of sports turf used in winter : a comparison of some rooting media with and without a gravel drainage layer. *J. Sports Turf Res. Inst.* **53**, 56-72.

Davis, W.B. (1983). Problems and solutions to maintaining sand greens and playing fields. *Calif. Turfgrass Culture* **33** (1, 2, 3 & 4), 1-2.

Davis, W.B., Paul, J.L., Madison, J.H. & George, L.Y. (1970). Evaluating sands and amendments used for high trafficked turf grass. *AXT n113, Agric. Extension Service,* Univ. Calif.

Hammond, L.K.F & Baker, S.W. (2002). The effects of sand type and rootzone amendments on green performance. IV. Water retention and turf quality under conditions of restricted irrigation. *J. Turfgrass & Sports Surface Sci.* **78**, 59-70.

Hunt, J.A. & Baker, S.W. (1996). The influence of rootzone depth and base construction on moisture retention profiles of sports turf rootzones. *J. Sports Turf Res. Inst.* **72**, 36-41.

Joo, Y.K., Lee, J.P., Christians, N.E. & Minner, D.D. (2001). Modification of sand-based soil media with organic and inorganic soil amendments. *Int. Turfgrass Soc. J.* **9**, 525-531.

Lawson, D.M. & Baker, S.W. (1987). The nutrient content of sands used for turf culture in the United Kingdom. *J. Sports Turf Res. Inst.* **63**, 49-56.

Li, D., Minner, D.D. & Christians, N.E. (2004). Quantitative evaluation of sand shape and roundness and their potential effect on stability of sand-based athletic fields. In: *Proc. 1st Int. Conf. Turfgrass Management & Science for Sports Fields*, Athens, Greece, 2-7 June 2003, pp. 159-170.

Madison, J.H. (1969). Sands used in soil mixes. *Calif. Turfgrass Culture* **19** (1), 3-5.

McCoy, E.L. (1992). Quantitative physical assessment of organic materials used in sports turf rootzone mixes. *Agron. J.* **84** (3), 375-381.

McCoy, E.L. (1998). Sand and organic amendment influences on soil physical properties related to turf establishment. *Agron. J.* **90**, 411-419.

McCoy, E.L. & Stehouwer, R.C. (1998). Water and nutrient retention properties of internally porous inorganic amendments in high sand content root zones. *J. Turfgrass Management* **2** (4), 49-69.

Murphy, J.W. & Nelson, S.H. (1979). Effects of turf on percolation and water holding capacity of three sand mixtures. *N.Z. J. Exp. Agric.* **7**, 245-248.

Murphy, J.W. & Nelson, S.H. (1979). Physical characteristics of particle size and distribution on Penncross bentgrass. *NZ J. Exp. Agric.* **7**, 249-255.

Paul, J.L. (1981). Fertility assay of sands. *Calif. Turfgrass Culture* **31** (1), 8-10.

Soil Survey (1974). *Soil Survey Field Handbook* (Ed. J.M. Hodgson). Soil Survey Technical Monograph No. 5, Harpenden, 99 pp.

Stewart, V.I. (1994). *Sports Turf—Science, Construction and Maintenance*. E. & F.N. Spon, London, 261 pp.

Swartz, W.E. & Kardos, L.T. (1963). Effect of compaction on physical properties of sand-soil-peat mixtures at various moisture contents. *Agron. J.* **55**, 7-10.

Taylor, D.H. & Blake, G.R. (1979). Sand content of sand-soil-peat mixtures for turfgrass. *Soil Sci. Soc. Amer. J.* **43** (2), 394-398.

Taylor, D.H. & Blake, G.R. (1981). Laboratory evaluation of soil mixtures for sports turf. *Soil Sci. Soc. Amer. J.* **45**, 936-40.

Taylor, D.H. & Blake, G.R. (1984). Predicting sand content of modified soil mixtures from sand-soil-peat properties. *Agron. J.* **76** (4), 583-87.

van Dam, J., Gibeault, V.A., Davis, W.B. & Meuller, K. (1975). A study of three sand mixes. *Calif. Turfgrass Culture* **25** (4), 25-27.

Waddington, D.V. (1976). Sands for modifying soils on turfgrass areas. *Pennsylvania Turfgrass Council Turfgrass Comments* **1** (1), 1 & 4.

Waddington, D.V. (1992). Soils, soil mixtures, and soil amendments. *Turfgrass Agron. Monograph No. 32*, pp. 331-383.

Waddington, D.V., Zimmerman, T.L., Shoop, G.J., Kardos, L.T. & Duich, J.M. (1974). Soil modification for turfgrass areas. *Pennsylvania State Univ. Agric. Exp. Sta. Progress Report 337*.

Ward, C.J. (1983). Sports turf drainage: a review. *J. Sports Turf Res. Inst.* **59**, 9-28.

Zhang, J. & Baker, S.W. (1999). Sand characteristics and their influence on the physical properties of rootzone mixes used for sports turf. *J. Turfgrass Sci.* **75**, 66-73.

Winter games pitches

Adams, W.A. (1986). Practical aspects of sports field drainage. *Soil Use & Management* **2** (2), 51-54.

Adams, W.A., Gibbs, R.J., Baker, S.W. & Lance, C.D. (1993). A national survey of winter games pitches in the UK with high quality drainage design. *Int. Turfgrass Soc. Res. J.* **7**, 405-412.

Adams, W.A., Stewart, V.I. & Thornton, D.J. (1971). The assessment of sands suitable for use in sportsfields. *J. Sports Turf Res. Inst.* **47**, 77-85.

Baker, S.W. (1988). Construction techniques for winter games pitches. In: *Science and Football, Proc. 1st World Congress of Science & Football*, Liverpool, England (Ed. T. Reilly *et al.*), pp. 399–405.

Baker, S.W. (1988). The effect of rootzone composition on the performance of winter games pitches III. Soil physical properties. *J. Sports Turf Res. Inst.* **64**, 133–143.

Baker, S.W. (1989). Soil physical conditions of the rootzone layer and the performance of winter games' pitches. *Soil Use and Management* **5** (3), 116-122.

Baker, S.W. (1991). Temporal variation of selected mechanical properties of natural turf football pitches. *J. Sports Turf Res. Inst.* **67**, 83-92.

Baker, S.W. (2004). Construction methods for public sector and professional sports pitches: A review. In: *Proc. 1st Int. Conf. Turfgrass Management & Science for Sports Fields*, Athens, Greece, June 2003, pp. 27-37.

Baker, S.W. & Canaway, P.M. (1990). The cost-effectiveness of different construction methods for Association Football pitches. I. Soil physical properties. *J. Sports Turf Res. Inst.* **66**, 8-20.

Baker, S.W. & Canaway, P.M. (1990). The effect of sand top dressing on the performance of winter games pitches of different construction types. I. Soil physical properties and ground cover. *J. Sports Turf Res. Inst.* **66**, 21-27.

Baker, S.W. & Canaway, P.M. (1991). The cost-effectiveness of different construction methods for Association Football pitches. II. Ground cover, playing quality and cost implications. *J. Sports Turf Res. Inst.* **67**, 53-65.

Baker, S.W. & Canaway, P.M. (1992). The effect of sand top dressing on the performance of winter games pitches of different construction types. II. Playing quality. *J. Sports Turf Res. Inst.* **68**, 62-72.

Baker, S.W. & Gibbs, R.J. (1989). Levels of use and the playing quality of winter games pitches of different construction types: case studies at Nottingham and Warrington. *J. Sports Turf Res. Inst.* **65**, 9-33.

Baker, S.W., Gibbs, R.J. & Adams, W.A. (1992). Case studies of the performance of different designs of winter games pitches. I. Playing quality and usage. *J. Sports Turf Res. Inst.* **68**, 20-32.

Baker, S.W. & Hacker, J.W. (1988). The use of peat in a Prunty-Mulqueen sand carpet construction: effects of application rate and depth. *J. Sports Turf Res. Inst.* **64**, 87-98.

Baker, S.W. & Isaac, S.P. (1987). The effect of rootzone composition on the performance of winter games pitches I. Sward characteristics. *J. Sports Turf Res. Inst.* **63**, 57-66.

Baker, S.W. & Isaac, S.P. (1987). The effect of rootzone composition on the performance of winter games pitches II. Playing quality. *J. Sports Turf Res. Inst.* **63**, 67-81.

DIN 18 035 (1978). Part 6. German DIN standard for sports grounds. Synthetic surface requirements, test, maintenance.

Dutch Working Group (1970). Werkgroep van de Nederlandse Sportfederatie en de Kon. Ned. Heidemaatschappij. De bruikbaarheid van zand bij de aanleg van sportvelden. *Tijdschr. Kon. Ned. Heidemij* **81** (12), 438-440.

Fisher, G.G. & Ede, A.N. (1974). Vertical band soil additive methods for established turf. In: *Proc. 2nd Int. Turfgrass Conf.*, pp. 281-286.

Gibbs, R.J. (2005). A practical model of assessment of sand carpet sports field condition and control of surface contamination. *Int. Turfgrass Soc. Res. J.* **10**, 347-355.

Gibbs, R.J., Adams, W.A. & Baker, S.W. (1993). Playing quality, performance and cost-effectiveness of soccer pitches in the UK. *Int. Turfgrass Soc. Res. J.* **7**, 212-221.

Gibbs, R.J., Adams, W.A. & Baker, S.W. (1992). Case studies of the performance of different designs of winter games pitches. II. Cost-effectiveness. *J. Sports Turf Res. Inst.* **68**, 33-49.

Gibbs, R.J., Adams, W.A. & Baker, S.W. (1993). Changes in soil physical properties of different construction methods for soccer pitches under intensive use. *Int. Turfgrass Soc. Res. J.* **7**, 413-421.

Gibbs, R.J. & Baker, S.W. (1989). Soil physical properties of winter games pitches of different construction types : case studies at Nottingham and Warrington. *J. Sports Turf Res. Inst.* **65**, 34-54.

Harper, J.C. (undated). *Athletic Fields. Specification, Outline, Construction and Maintenance.* Pennsylvania State University, 29 pp.

Holmes, G. & Bell, M.J. (1987). Variations in the playing quality of different soccer pitch constructions. *Z. für Vegetationstechnik* **10**, 83-88.

Macolino, S., Recchia, F., Scotton, M. & Ziliotto, U. (2004). Effect of simulated traffic on some substrate physical parameters in construction systems of soccer pitches. In: *Proc. 1st Int. Conf. Turfgrass Management & Science for Sports Fields*, Athens, Greece, June 2003, pp. 171-175.

Magni, S., Volterrani, M. & Miele, S. (2004). Soccer pitches performance as affected by construction method, sand type and turfgrass mixture. In: *Proc. 1st Int. Conf. Turfgrass Management & Science for Sports Fields*, Athens, Greece, June 2003, pp. 281-285.

Mulqueen, J. (1976). Aspects of construction of sports fields and recreation grounds in Ireland. In: *The Next Decade in Amenity Grassland* (Ed. C.E. Wright), Queen's Univ. Press, Belfast, pp. 40-65.

Petersen, M. (1974). Construction of sportsgrounds based on physical soil characteristics. In: *Proc. 2nd Int. Turfgrass Res. Conf.*, Blacksburg, Virginia, USA (Ed. E.C. Roberts), pp. 270-276.

Reyneri, A. & Bruno, G. (2004). The effects of wear on three soils and two turfgrass mixtures for soccer grounds. In: *Proc. 1st Int. Conf. Turfgrass Management & Science for Sports Fields*, Athens, Greece,June 2003, pp. 49-52.

Skirde, W. (1973). Soil modification for sports turf playing surfaces. *Rasen Turf Gazon* **2**, 21-24.

Skirde, W. (1974). Soil modification for athletic fields. In: *Proc. 2nd Int. Turfgrass Res. Conf.*, Blacksburg, Virginia, USA (Ed. E.C. Roberts), pp. 261-269.

Skirde, W. (1989). Problems and research on sports turf areas in West Germany, with particular reference to the deterioration in environmental conditions. In: *Proc. 6th Int. Turfgrass Res. Conf.*, Japanese Soc. Turfgrass Science, Tokyo (Ed. H. Takatoh), pp. 29-35.

STRI (1994). *Winter Games Pitches—The Construction and Maintenance of Natural Turf Pitches for Team Games* (Ed. R.D.C. Evans). Sports Turf Research Institute, 209 pp.

The Sports Turf Association (1991). *An Athletic Field Managers' Guide for Construction and Maintenance*. Sport Turf Association, Ontario, 39 pp.

Thornton, D.J. (1973). A field trial of sports field construction materials extremely high in sand content. *J. Sports Turf Res. Inst.* **49**, 29-44.

van Wijk, A.L.M. (1980). *A soil technological study on effectuating and maintaining adequate playing conditions of grass sports fields*. Agric. Res. Rep. 903, Centre for Agricultural Publishing and Documentation, Wageningen, The Netherlands, 124 pp.

van Wijk, A.L.M. (1980). Soil water conditions and the playability of grass sports fields. I. Influence of soil physical properties of top layer and subsoil. *Z. für Vegetationstechnik* **3** (1), 7-15.

van Wijk, A.L.M. (1980). Soil water conditions and the playability of grass sports fields. II. Influence of tile drainage and sandy drainage layer. *Z. für Vegetationstechnik* **3** (1), 16-22.

Golf

Australian Golf Union & The Australian Turfgrass Research Insitute Ltd (1995). *Bunker sand specification for Australian Golf Courses—Summary of Key Results.*

Baker, S.W. (1991). Rootzone composition and the performance of golf greens. I. Sward characteristics before and after the first year of simulated wear. *J. Sports Turf Res. Inst.* **67**, 14-23.

Baker, S.W. & Binns, D.J. (2001). Vertical distribution of moisture in golf greens following gravitational drainage: the effects of intermediate layer and drainage layer materials. *Int. Turfgrass Society Res. J.* **9**, 463-468.

Baker, S.W. & Beggs, A.J. (1995). The construction and maintenance of bunkers. In: *Golf. The Scientific Way.* (Ed. A. Cochran), Aston Publishing Group, pp. 276-279.

Baker, S.W., Binns, D.J. & Cook, A. (1997). Performance of sand-dominated golf greens in relation to rootzone characteristics. *J. Turfgrass Sci.* **73**, 43-57.

Baker, S.W., Cole, A.R, & Thornton, S.L. (1990). The effect of sand type on ball impacts, angle of repose and stability of footing in golf bunkers. In: *Science and Golf, Proc. 1st World Scientific Congress of Golf*, University of St. Andrews (Ed. A.J. Cochran), July, pp. 352-357, E. & F.N. Spon.

Baker, S.W., Mooney, S.J. & Cook, A. (1999). The effects of sand type and rootzone amendments on golf green performance. I. Soil properties *J. Turfgrass Sci.* **75**, 2-17.

Baker, S.W., Mooney, S.J. & Cook, A. (1999). The effects of sand type and rootzone amendments on golf green performance. II. Grass characteristics. *J. Turfgrass Sci.* **75**, 18-26.

Baker, S.W., Mooney, S.J. & Cook, A. (1999). The effects of sand type and rootzone amendments on golf green performance. III. Playing quality. *J. Turfgrass Sci.* **75**, 27-35.

Baker, S.W. & Richards, C.W. (1991). Rootzone composition and the performance of golf greens. II. Playing quality under conditions of simulated wear. *J. Sports Turf Res. Inst.* **67**, 24-31.

Baker, S.W. & Richards, C.W. (1993). Rootzone composition and the performance of golf greens. III. Soil physical properties. *J. Sports Turf Res. Inst.* **69**, 38-48.

Baker, S.W. & Richards, C.W. (1995). The effect of rootzone composition on the playing quality of *Festuca/Agrostis/Poa annua* golf greens. *J. Turfgrass Management* **1** (3), 53-68.

Baker, S.W. & Richards, C.W. (1997). Soil physical properties of golf greens: relationships between laboratory and field measurements. *Int. Turfgrass Soc. Res. J.* **8**, 47-58.

Baker, S.W., Richards, C.W. & Cook, A. (1997). Rootzone composition and the performance of golf greens. IV. Changes in botanical composition over a four year period from grass establishment. *J. Turfgrass Sci.* **73**, 30-42.

Baker, S.W. (2003). Management of Dutch Golf Greens and Possible Responses to Monitoring Information. Netherlandse Golf Federatie Report, 21 pp.

Bigelow, C.A., Bowman, D.D. & Cassel, D.K. (2001). Water retention of sand-based putting green mixtures as affected by the presence of gravel sub-layers. *Int. Turfgrass Soc. J.* **9**, 479-486.

Brown, K.W. & Duble, R.L. (1975). Physical characteristics of soil mixtures used for golf green construction. *Agron. J.* **67** (5), 647-652.

Brown, K.W. & Thomas, J.C. (1980). The influence of sand layer on available water retention in a golf green. *USGA Green Section Record* **18** (6), 80.

Brown, K.W. & Thomas, J.C. (1986). Bunker sand selection. *Golf Course Management,* July, pp. 64-70.

Brown, K.W., Thomas, J.C. & Almodares, A. (1980). The necessity of the two-inch sand layer in greens construction. *USGA Green Section Record* **18** (6), 80.

Cook, A. & Baker, S.W. (1998). Effects of organic amendments on selected physical and chemical properties of rootzones for golf greens. *J. Turfgrass Sci.* **74,** 2-10.

Cook, A. & Baker, S.W. (1998). Organic amendments for sand-dominated golf green rootzones. In: *Science and Golf III. Proc. World Scientific Congress of Golf,* St. Andrews, pp. 637-646.

Collinge, J. (1997). Golf in the Netherlands. *Int. Turfgrass Bulletin* **195**, 14-17.

Cooper, R.J. & Skogley, C.R. (1981) An evaluation of several top dressing programs for *Agrostis palustis Huds.* and *Agrostis canina* L. putting green turf. In: *Proc 4th Int. Turfgrass Res. Conf.*, Ontario Agric. College/Int. Turfgrass Soc. (Ed. R.W. Sheard), pp. 129-136.

Cooper, R.J. & Skogley, C.R. (1981). Putting green responses to sand and sand-soil top dressing. *USGA Green Section Record* **19** (3), 9-13.

Davis, W.B. (1973). Examples of real solutions—the fine sand green. *Calif.*

Turfgrass Culture **23** (3), 20-24.

Davis, W.B. (1973). Sands and their place on the golf course. *Calif. Turfgrass Culture* **23** (3), 17-20.

Davis, W.B. (1977). Sands and your putting green. *Calif. Turfgrass Culture* **27** (4), 31-32.

Davis, W.B. (1978). Pros and cons of frequent sand top dressing. *Calif. Turfgrass Culture* **28** (4), 25-29.

Davis, W.B. (1981). Sand green construction. *Calif. Turfgrass Culture* **31** (1), 4-7.

Dixon, C.R. (1992). Sands for bunkers. *Grounds Maintenance*, January, pp. 71-73.

Frank, K.W., Leach, B.E., Crum, J.R., Rieke, P.E., Leinauer, B.R., Nikolai, T.A. & Calhoun, R.N. (2005). The effects of a variable depth root zone on soil moisture in a sloped USGA putting green. *Int. Turfgrass Soc. J.* **10**, 1060-66.

Gibbs, R.J., Lui, C., Yang, M-H. & Wrigley, M.P. (2001). Effect of rootzone composition and cultivation/aeration treatment on the physical and root growth performance of golf greens under New Zealand conditions. *Int. Turfgrass Soc. J.* **9**, 506-517.

Hammond, L.K.F & Baker, S.W. (2002). The effects of sand type and rootzone amendments on green performance. IV. Water retention and turf quality under conditions of restricted irrigation. *J. Turfgrass & Sports Surface Sci.* **78**, 59-70.

Hannaford, J. & Baker, S.W. (2000). The effect of rootzone composition and compaction on root development in sand-dominated golf greens. *J. Turfgrass Sci.* **76**, 24-36.

Hind, P.D., Baker, S.W., Lodge, T.A., Hunt, J.A. & Binns, D.J. (1995). A survey of golf greens in Great Britain. I. Soil properties. *J. Sports Turf Res. Inst.* **71**, 9-22.

Hummel, N.W. (1993). Rationale for the revisions of the USGA green construction specifications. *USGA Green Section Record*, March/April, pp. 7-21.

Hummel, N.W. (1993). Laboratory methods for evaluation of putting green rootzone mixes. *USGA Green Section Record*, March/April, pp. 23-33.

Hummel, N (1994). Revisiting the USGA green recommendations. *Golf Course Management*, July, pp. 57-59.

Lodge, T.A. & Baker, S.W. (1991). The construction, irrigation and fertiliser nutrition of golf greens. II. Playing quality assessments after establishment and during the first year of differential irrigation and nutrition treatments *J. Sports Turf Res. Inst.* **67**, 44-52.

Lodge, T.A. & Baker, S.W. (1993). Porosity, moisture release characteristics and infiltration rates of three golf green rootzones. *J. Sports Turf Res. Inst.* **69**, 49-58.

Lodge, T.A., Baker, S.W., Canaway, P.M. & Lawson, D.M. (1991). The construction, irrigation and fertiliser nutrition of golf greens. I. Botanical and reflectance assessments after establishment and during the first year of differential irrigation and nutrition treatments. *J. Sports Turf Res. Inst.* **67**, 32-43.

Lunt, O.R. (1956). A method for minimising compaction in putting greens. *S. Calif. Turfgrass Culture* **6** (3), 1-4.

Marshall, R.I. & Lindsay, M.R. (1990). A comparative study of the properties of bunker sands from links and championship golf courses in Great Britain and Ireland. In: *Science and Golf. Proc. 1st World Scientific Congress of Golf,* Univ. of St. Andrews (Ed. A.J. Cochran), July, pp. 346-351, E. & F.N. Spon.

Morgan, W.C. (1974). Report of sand-organic mixes for putting green construction. In: *Proc. 2nd Int. Turfgrass Res. Conf.,* Blacksburg, Virginia, USA (Ed. E.C. Roberts), p. 298.

Murphy, J.A., Honig, J.A., Samaranayake, H., Lawson, T.J. & Murphy, S.L. (2001). Creeping bentgrass establishment on root zones varying in sand sizes. *Int. Turfgrass Soc. J.* **9**, 573-579.

Murphy, J.A., Samaranayake, H., Honig, J.A., Lawson, T.J. & Murphy, S.L. (2005). Creeping bentgrass establishment on amended-sand root zones in two microenvironments. *Crop Sci.* **45**, 1511-1520.

Neyland, J. & Robinson, M. (1997). Sand amendments for turf construction. *Int. Turfgrass Soc. Res. J.* **8**, 133-147.

O'Brien, P.M. & Ferguson, M.H. (1983). Selection and handling sand. *USGA Green Section Record,* November/December, pp. 1-4.

O'Brien, P.M. (1985). Choosing bunker sands. *Golf Course Management,* August, pp. 56-63.

Owen, A.G., Hammond, L.K.F. & Baker, S.W. (2005). Examination of the physical properties of recycled glass-derived sands for use in golf green rootzones. *Int. Turfgrass Soc. Res. J.* **10**, 1131-1137.

Owen, A.G., Woollacott, A.R. & Baker, S.W. (2005). An evaluation of recycled glass-derived sand for use in golf course bunkers. *Int. Turfgrass Soc. Res. J.* **10**, 1138-1143.

Prettyman, G. & McCoy, E. (1999). Subsurface drainage of modern putting greens. *USGA Green Section Record,* July/August, pp. 12-15.

Prettyman, G.W. & McCoy, E.L. (2003). Profile layering, root zone permeability, and slope affect on soil water content during putting green drainage. *Crop Sci.* **43**, 985-994.

Radko, A.M. (1974). Refining green section specifications for putting green construction. In: *Proc. 2nd Int. Turfgrass Res. Conf.*, Blacksburg, Virginia, USA (Ed. E.C. Roberts), pp. 287-297.

Radko, A.M. & Bengeyfield (1975). The agronomics of course preparation for major championships. *USGA Green Section Record* **13**, 1-5.

Richardson, M.D. & Karcher, D.E. (2001). Addition of inorganic amendments to a mature, sand-based putting green. *Int. Turfgrass Soc. J.* **9**, 610-614.

Schmidt, R.E. (1980). Bentgrass growth in relation to soil properties of typic Hapludalfs soil variously modified for a golf green. In: *Proc. 3rd Int. Turfgrass Res. Conf.*, Munich, Germany (Ed. J.B. Beard), pp. 205-214.

STRI (1996). *The Care of the Golf Course* (Eds. J. Perris & R.D.C. Evans). Sports Turf Research Institute, 340 pp.

STRI (2005). *Golf Green Construction in the United Kingdom*. Sports Turf Research Institute, 20 pp.

Taylor, D.H., Nelson, S.D. & Williams, C.F. (1993). Sub-rootzone layering effects on water retention in sports turf soil profiles. *Agron. J.* **85**, 626-630.

USGA Green Section Staff (1974). Sand for golf courses. *USGA Green Section Record*, September, pp. 12-13.

USGA Green Section Staff (2004). USGA recommendations for a method of putting green construction. *USGA Green Section website, www.usga.org*

Waltz Jr., F.C. & McCarty, L.B. (2005). Field evaluation of soil amendments used in rootzone mixes for golf course putting greens. *Int. Turfgrass Soc. J.* **10**, 1150-1158.

Wilson, C.G. (1968). The correct sand for putting greens. *Calif. Turfgrass Culture* **18** (4), 31-32.

Bowling greens

Baker, S.W. & Richards, C.W. (1993). The effect of rootzone composition and surface moisture content on the speed of bowling greens. *J. Sports Turf Res. Inst.* **69**, 31-37.

Davis, W.B. (1977). Soils and sands for bowling greens. *Calif. Turfgrass Culture* **27** (3), 19-20.

Evans, R.D.C. (1992). *Bowling Greens: Their History, Construction and Maintenance*. Sports Turf Research Institute, Bingley, 211 pp.

Cricket

Adams, W.A. (1983). Guidelines on buying cricket topdressings. *Turf Management* **2** (10), 11.

Adams, W.A., Baker, S.W., Carre , M.J., Young, R.J. & James, D.M. (2004). P*itch Properties and Performance*. England & Wales Cricket Board, 16 pp.

Adams, W.A., Baker, S.W, James, D.M. & Young, R.J. (2005). Measuring and modelling the bounce and pace of county championship cricket pitches. *Int. Turfgrass Soc. Res. J.* **10**, 1021-1026.

Adams, W.A. &. Young, R.J. (2001). Laboratory testing of the friction characteristics of novel mixes for cricket pitch rootzones. *Int. Turfgrass Soc. Res. J.* **9**, 445-450.

Adams, W.A., Young, R.J. & Baker, S.W. (2001). Some soil and turf factors affecting playing characteristics of premier cricket pitches in the UK. *Int. Turfgrass Soc. Res. J.* **9**, 451-457.

Arundell, P.A. & Baker, S.W. (1984). Photomicrographic examination of soil conditions of problem pitches at two County grounds in England. *J. Sports Turf Res. Inst.* **60**, 54-60.

Baker, S.W., Binns, D.J., Cook, A. & Mooney, S.J. (2001). The performance of cricket pitches in relation to soil type and moisture content. *Int. Turfgrass Society Res. J.* **9**, 469-478.

Baker, S.W., Cook, A. & Adams, W.A. (1998). Soil characteristics of first-class cricket pitches and their influence on playing performance. *J. Turfgrass Sci.* **74**, 63-79.

Baker, S.W., Cook, A. & Binns, D.J. (1998). The effect of soil type and profile construction on the performance of cricket pitches. I. Soil properties and grass cover during the first season of use. *J. Turfgrass Sci.* **74**, 80-92.

Baker, S.W., Cook, A., Binns, D.J., Carr , M.J. & Haake, S.J. (1998). The effect of soil type and profile construction on the performance of cricket pitches. II. Playing quality during the first season of use. *J. Turfgrass Sci.* **74**, 93-107.

Baker, S.W., Hammond, L.K.F., Owen, A.G. & Adams, W.A. (2003). Soil physical properties of first class cricket pitches in England and Wales: I. Classification system for soil characteristics. *J. Turfgrass & Sports Surface Sci.* **78**, 2-12.

Baker, S.W., Hammond, L.K.F., Owen, A.G. & Adams, W.A. (2003). Soil physical properties of first class cricket pitches in England and Wales: II. Influence of soil type and pitch preparation on playing quality. *J. Turfgrass & Sports Surface Sci.* **78**, 13-22.

Baker, S.W., Isaac, S.P. & Isaac, B.J. (1988). The playing performance of cricket pitches in relation to the depth of heavy loam material. *J. Sports Turf Res. Inst.* **64**, 170-176.

Baker, S.W. & Woollacott, A.R. (2005). Construction profiles of cricket pitches and their effect on soil characteristics and playing performance. *Int. Turfgrass Soc. Res. J.* **10**, 1034-1041.

Cameron-Lee, S.P. & McAuliffe, K.W. (1989). Evaluating the Adams and Stewart soil binding test for cricket pitch soil selection. In: *Proc. 6th Int. Turfgrass Conf.* (Ed. H. Takatoh), Int. Turfgrass Soc./Japanese Soc. Turfgrass Sci., pp. 193-196.

Carre, M.J., Baker, S.W., Newell, A.J. & Haake, S.J. (1999). The dynamic behaviour of cricket balls during impact and variations due to grass and soil type. *Sports Engineering* **2**, 145-160.

English Cricket Board (undated). *Recommended Guidelines for the Preparation and Maintenance of Cricket Pitches and Outfields at all Levels of the Game.* English and Wales Cricket Board, 47 pp.

Evans, R.D.C. (1991). Cricket Grounds. *The Evolution, Maintenance and Construction of Natural Turf Cricket Tables and Outfields.* Sports Turf Research Institute, 221 pp.

Evans, R.D.C. (1996). *The Cricket Groundsman's Companion. A Basic Guide to the Maintenance of Cricket Tables and Outfields.* Sports Turf Research Institute/ Tildenet, 20 pp.

Harris, J.R. (1961). The crumbling of cricket pitches. *Australian Scientist* **1**, 173-178.

Kemp, R.A. (1994). Soil micromorphology of local authority cricket tables. *Soil Use & Management* **10**, 65-71.

Lush, W.M., Cummings, D.J. & McIntyre, D.S. (1985). Turf cricket wickets. *Search* **16**, 142-45.

McAuliffe, K.W. & Gibbs, R.J. (1997). An investigation of the pace and bounce of cricket pitches in New Zealand. *Int. Turfgrass Soc. Res. J.* **8**, 109-119.

McAuliffe, K.W. & Hannan, B.K. (2001). Effects of root zone construction and preparation methods on cricket pitch performance. *Int. Turfgrass Soc. Res. J.* **9**, 553-558.

Murphy, J.W. & Field, T.R.O. (1991). Factors affecting pace on New Zealand cricket pitches. *NZ Turf Man. J.*, pp. 15-19.

Stewart, V.I. & Adams, W.A. (1968). County cricket wickets. *J. Sports Turf Res. Inst.* **44**, 49-60.

Stewart, V.I. & Adams, W.A. (1969). Soil factors affecting the control of pace on cricket wickets. In: *Proc. 1st Int. Turfgrass Res. Conf.*, Harrogate, England, pp. 533-546. Sports Turf Res. Inst./Int. Turfgrass Soc.

Walmsley, B. (1997). Soil density, moisture and elevation changes during cricket pitch preparation. *NZ Turf Man. J.* **11** (2), 5-10.

Tennis

McClements, I. (2000). Top dressing. In: *Grass Tennis Courts—How to Construct and Maintain Them* (Ed. J. Perris). Sports Turf Research Institute/All England Lawn Tennis Club, Wimbledon, pp. 89-92.

Pool, S.T. (2000). Design and construction of tennis courts. In: *Grass Tennis Courts—How to Construct and Maintain Them* (Ed. J. Perris). Sports Turf Research Institute/All England Lawn Tennis Club, Wimbledon, pp. 28-37.

Appendix I
Soil Testing by Accredited Laboratories

Laboratory test results are of limited value if the testing is not carried out to a high standard and fully in accordance with a recognised test procedure. For testing of sports turf rootzones, the most widely accepted form of accreditation is through the American Association for Laboratory Accreditation (A2LA).

THE AMERICAN
ASSOCIATION
FOR LABORATORY
ACCREDITATION

ACCREDITED LABORATORY

A2LA has accredited

SPORTS TURF RESEARCH INSTITUTE
West Yorkshire, ENGLAND

for technical competence in the field of

Geotechnical (Putting Green Materials) Testing

The accreditation covers the specific tests and types of tests listed on the agreed scope of accreditation. This laboratory meets the requirements of ISO/IEC 17025 - 1999 "General Requirements for the Competence of Testing and Calibration Laboratories" and any additional program requirements in the identified field of testing.

Presented this 6th day of July 2005.

President
For the Accreditation Council
Certificate Number 2159.01
Valid to July 31, 2007

For tests or types of tests to which this accreditation applies,
please refer to the laboratory's Geotechnical Scope of Accreditation.
REPRINT

Under this scheme, laboratories will be checked for compliance with the relevant test procedures, have equipment and calibration procedures that can be traced to national standards, have detailed documentation for sample control and will participate in a proficiency scheme so that results from standard samples can be compared with those from other laboratories. For sports turf rootzones, laboratories participate in the USGA Green Section Proficiency Testing programme.

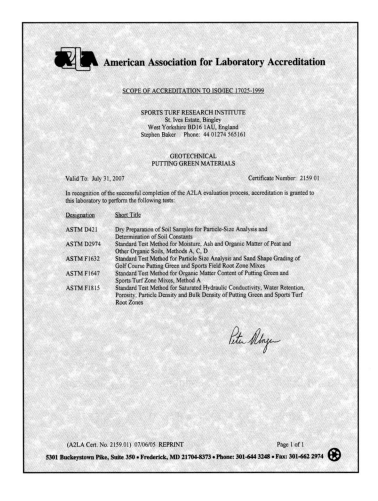

American Association for Laboratory Accreditation

SCOPE OF ACCREDITATION TO ISO/IEC 17025-1999

SPORTS TURF RESEARCH INSTITUTE
St. Ives Estate, Bingley
West Yorkshire BD16 1AU, England
Stephen Baker   Phone: 44 01274 565161

GEOTECHNICAL
PUTTING GREEN MATERIALS

Valid To: July 31, 2007   Certificate Number: 2159.01

In recognition of the successful completion of the A2LA evaluation process, accreditation is granted to this laboratory to perform the following tests:

Designation	Short Title
ASTM D421	Dry Preparation of Soil Samples for Particle-Size Analysis and Determination of Soil Constants
ASTM D2974	Standard Test Method for Moisture, Ash and Organic Matter of Peat and Other Organic Soils, Methods A, C, D
ASTM F1632	Standard Test Method for Particle Size Analysis and Sand Shape Grading of Golf Course Putting Green and Sports Field Root Zone Mixes
ASTM F1647	Standard Test Method for Organic Matter Content of Putting Green and Sports Turf Zone Mixes, Method A
ASTM F1815	Standard Test Method for Saturated Hydraulic Conductivity, Water Retention, Porosity, Particle Density and Bulk Density of Putting Green and Sports Turf Root Zones

(A2LA Cert. No. 2159.01) 07/06/05 REPRINT   Page 1 of 1

5301 Buckeystown Pike, Suite 350 • Frederick, MD 21704-8373 • Phone: 301-644 3248 • Fax: 301-662 2974

List of Sand, Rootzone and Top Dressing Suppliers

The following companies are all sand, rootzone and top dressing suppliers in the United Kingdom and Ireland and have kindly contributed to the costs of producing this book. For convenience, companies are listed in two sections, those specialising in sands and sand-dominated top dressings and those dealing with the heavier soils used for cricket and tennis.

Sand and Sand-dominated Rootzone/Top Dressing Suppliers

Aitkens, 123 Harmony Row, Glasgow G51 3NB
Contact: Mr Richard Aitken • Tel: 0141 440 0033 • Fax: 0141 440 2733
Email: enquiries@aitkens.co.uk • Web: www.aitkens.co.uk

Bailey's of Norfolk Ltd, Brick Kiln Road, Hevingham, Norfolk NR10 5NL
Contact: Mr John Farrell • Tel: 01603 754607 • Fax: 01603 754147
Email: info@baileysofnorfolk.co.uk • Web: www.baileysofnorfolk.co.uk

Banks Amenity Products Ltd, 4 The Point Business Park, Rockingham Road, Market Harborough, Leicestershire LE16 7QU
Contact: Mrs Sarah Farmer • Tel: 01858 464346 • Fax: 01858 433003
Email: enquiries@banksamenity.co.uk • Web: www.banksamenity.co.uk

Bathgate Silica Sand Ltd, Arclid Quarry, Congleton Road, Sandbach, Cheshire CW11 4SN
Contact: Mr Nick Gray • Tel: 01270 762828 • Fax: 01270 760557
Email: sales@bathgatesilica.co.uk • Web: www.bathgatesilica.co.uk

Bourne Amenity Ltd, The Whark, Newenden, Cranbrook, Kent TN18 5QG
Contact: Mr David Kirby • Tel: 01797 252299 • Fax: 01797 253115
Email: david@bourne.co.uk • Web: www.bourneamenity.co.uk

Bucbricks Company Ltd, Martells Quarry, Slough Lane, Ardleigh, Essex
CO7 7RU
Contact: Ms Vanessa Ingram ● Tel: 01206 230310 ● Fax: 01206 231057
Email: enquiries@bucbricks.co.uk ● Web: www.bucbricks.com

Garside Sands, Eastern Way, Leighton Buzzard, Bedfordshire LU7 9LF
Contact: Liz Boon ● Tel: 01525 237911 ● Fax: 01535 237991
Email: garside.sands@aggregate.com ● Web: www.garside-sands.com

Goonvean Aggregates, St Stephen, St Austell, Cornwall PL26 7QF
Contact: Mr Nick Ellery ● Tel: 01726 822381 ● Fax: 01726 822341
Email: nellery@goonvean.co.uk ● Web: www.goonvean.co.uk

Hugh King & Co, Hullerhill Sand Quarry, Kilwinning, North Ayrshire KA13 7QN
Contact: Mr Graeme King ● Tel: 01294 557515 ● Fax: 01294 557523
Email: graeme@hughking.co.uk ● Web: www.hughking.co.uk

Mansfield Sand & Fibresand UK Ltd, Sandhurst Ave, Mansfield,
Nottinghamshire NG18 4BE
Contact: Dr V.J. Armond ● Tel: 01623 622441 ● Fax: 01623 420904
Email: vja@mansfield-sand.co.uk ● Web: www.mansfieldsand.co.uk

Monro Sport, Unit 18-20 Enstone Airfield Industrial Estate, Enstone,
Oxfordshire OX7 4NP
Contact: Mr Alan Ford ● Tel: 0870 242 1090 ● Fax: 0870 242 1091
Email: enstonesales@monrosouth.co.uk ● Web: www.monrosouth.co.uk

Monro Sport, Moreton, Ongar, Essex CM5 0HY
Contact: Mr Philip Furner ● Tel: 01277 890246 ● Fax: 01277 890105
Email: sales@binderloams.co.uk ● Web: www.binderloams.co.uk

Natural World Products Ltd, 55 Cargallougher Road, Keady, Co. Armagh
BT60 3RA
Contact: Mr Alastair Dunwoody ● Tel: 028 3753 1591 ● Fax: 028 3753 9426
Email: alastair.dunwoody@nwp-recylce.com ● Web: www.roseylee.com /
www.nwp-recycle.com

Northstone (NI) Ltd, 7 Creagh Road, Toomebridge, Co. Antrim BT41 3SD
Contact: Mr Keith Wood ● Tel: 028 7965 0461 ● Fax: 028 7965 0238
Email: sales@northstone-ni.com ● Web: www.northstone-ni.com

Sporting Surface Supplies Ltd, Hurstridge, Hathersham Lane, Smallfield,
Surrey RH6 9JG
Contact: Ms Sophi Rumble ● Tel: 01342 843663 ● Fax: 01342 844180
Email: info@sportingsurfacesupplies.com ● Web: www.sportingsurfacesupplies.com

Tinto Sand & Gravel Ltd, Tinto Quarry, Thankerton, Biggar, Lanarkshire
ML12 6NJ
Contact: Mr Douglas MacKenzie ● Tel: 01899 308372 ● Fax: 01899 308372

Topsport, Eaton Hall Quarry, Manchester Road, Congleton, Cheshire
CW12 2LU
Contact: Mr John Halfpenny ● Tel: 01260 275214 ● Fax: 01260 299149
Email: topsport@tarmac.co.uk ● Web: www.topsport.co.uk

WBB Minerals, Brookside Hall, Sandbach, Cheshire CW11 4TF
Contact: Mr David Robb ● Tel: 07836 705493 ● Fax: 01270 752753
Email: dave.robb@wbbminerals.com ● Web: www.wbbminerals.com

W D Irwin & Sons Ltd, 55 Gortgonis Road, Coalisland, County Tyrone
BT71 4QG
Contact: Mr Alastair Harrison ● Tel: 028 8774 0362 ● Fax: 028 8774 7473
Email: sales@irwin-aggregates.com ● Web: www.irwin-aggregates.com

White Moss Amenities Ltd, Business & Technology Centre, Radway Green
Venture Park, Alsager, Cheshire CW2 5PR
Contact: Sharon Law ● Tel: 01270 886266 ● Fax: 01270 886294
Email: info@wes-ltd.com ● Web: www.wes-ltd.com

Yorkshire Aggregates Quarrying Ltd, Wroot Road Quarry, Wroot Road,
Finningley, Doncaster, South Yorkshire DN9 3DU
Contact: Mr Andy Burton ● Tel: 01302 770500 ● Fax: 01302 772502
Email: andy@yaql.biz ● Web: www.yaql.biz

Cricket/Tennis Loam Suppliers

Binder Loams, Embleys Farm, Moreton, Ongar, Essex CM5 0HY
Contact: Mr Philip Furner ● Tel: 01277 890246 ● Fax: 01277 890105
Email: sales@binderloams.co.uk ● Web: www.binderloams.co.uk

Boughton Loam Ltd, Telford Way Industrial Estate, Kettering, Northants NN16 8UN
Contact: Mr Simon Hedley ● Tel: 01536 510515 ● Fax: 01536 510691
Email: shedley@boughton-loam.co.uk ● Web: www.boughton-loam.co.uk

Bourne Amenity Ltd, The Whark, Newenden, Cranbrook, Kent TN18 5QG
Contact: Mr David Kirby ● Tel: 01797 252299 ● Fax: 01797 253115
Email: david@bourne.co.uk ● Web: www.bourneamenity.co.uk

G.S.B. Loams Ltd, PO BOX 66, Kettering, Northants NN14 1RT
Contact: Mr David Goodjohn ● Tel: 01536 791155 ● Fax: 01536 790433
Email: info@gsbloams.co.uk ● Web: www.gsbloams.co.uk

Monro Sport, Unit 18-20 Enstone Airfield Industrial Estate, Enstone, Oxfordshire OX7 4NP
Contact: Ms Debbie Atkinson ● Tel: 0870 242 1090 ● Fax: 0870 242 1091
Email: enstonesales@monrosouth.co.uk ● Web: www.monrosouth.co.uk

Natural World Products Ltd, 55 Cargallougher Road, Keady, Co. Armagh BT60 3RA
Contact: Mr Alastair Dunwoody ● Tel: 028 3753 1591 ● Fax: 028 3753 9426
Email: alastair.dunwoody@nwp-recylce.com ● Web: www.roseylee.com / www.nwp-recycle.com

Sporting Surface Supplies Ltd, Hurstridge, Hathersham Lane, Smallfield, Surrey RH6 9JG
Contact: Ms Sophi Rumble ● Tel: 01342 843663 ● Fax: 01342 844180
Email: info@sportingsurfacesupplies.com ● Web: www.sportingsurfacesupplies.com

British Rootzone & Top Dressing Manufacturers Association

BRTMA was established in 2000 to represent the interests of producers of quality construction mixes and top dressings. Our member companies offer approved, repeatable and quality controlled products for the construction and maintenance of sports turf areas. STRI is our appointed testing house, ensuring that materials from all the member companies are tested along identical lines.

What does BRTMA membership mean?

- All members' products are tested on a regular basis using standardised procedures.
- All members comply with the BRTMA Quality Management Scheme
- BRTMA promotes the use of appropriate materials and offers the best working practices in manufacture in order to offer a consistent and repeatable standard
- BRTMA members promote materials offered within a quality framework
- The Association is committed to developing the use of environmentally friendly products
- The Association is promoting research into effective UK rootzone specifications
- The Association works with other organisations involved in the specification and purchase of Rootzones and Top Dressings

Our Members

Bailey's of Norfolk
Banks Amenity Products Ltd
Bathgate Silica Sand Ltd
Boughton Loam
Bourne Amenity
Garside Sands
Mansfield Sand
Pro-Sport (WBB Minerals)
Roffey Ltd
Rufford Sport Surface Technology
Tarmac Topsport
Whitemoss Amenities

For contact details please see individual entries in this book or visit www.brtma.com

Yorkshire Aggregates Quarrying Limited

Leading suppliers of :

TURF DRESSINGS

- T73D Dressing
- Swardsman Dressing
- Pro Dressing
- Nutrient Enhanced Dressings

ROOTZONE

- Rootzone Standard
- Rootzone Plus
- Rootzone Ultra

Bunker Sands

Dressing Sands

Sterilised Topsoil

Green Waste Fairways Dressings

Decorative Aggregates

Drainage Materials

Pathway Materials

Appointed distributors in the north of England for

NutriMate Limited

NutriMate is a completely new concept in nutrient management and greatly increases the efficiency of all fertilizers.

Ideal for sand construction

With a CEC of up to 280meq per litre generated from the Humic acid molecule when incorporated into soils greatly reduces any leaching and ensures maximum nutrient use from every application of fertilizer

Fulvic acid present in the mineral is an excellent organic chelator of all plant nutrients and promotes dramatic increases in both sward density and root depth and bio mass.

NutriMate Limited produce a full range of quality granular and liquid fertilizers incorporating either the mineral into the granular fertilizers or NutriMate amenity liquid high in fulvic acid into all the liquid range with dramatic effect.

Better colour

Improved drought resistance

Longer lasting nutrient applications

Faster rooting of all turf

Faster establishment of all seed

Superb sward density

Improved disease resistance

Wroot Road Quarry
Wroot Road
Finningley
Doncaster
South Yorkshire

Available in
BULK LOADS—30, 20, 16 & 10 TONNE
1 TONNE BULK BAG
25kg PRE PACK BAG

Phone: : 01302 770500
Fax: : 01302 772502
Email : sales@yaql.biz
Website : www.yaql.biz

The Sports Turf Research Institute

The Sports Turf Research Institute (STRI) is an independent, non-profit organisation whose objectives are to carry out research and to provide advice and education in the sphere of sports turf. The Institute has its origins in 1929 when the "Board of Greenkeeping Research" was founded by The Royal and Ancient Golf Club of St. Andrews and the four Home Golf Unions to carry out research and to provide advice and education on matters relating to golf turf. In time, it was found that owners and managers of other sports areas also required advice on their turf problems. In recognition of this wider need, in 1951 the STRI was incorporated as a much more broadly based organisation with most of the sports governing bodies being in membership and able to influence policy through their representation on the Board of Management.

As an independent body, the STRI is free to offer an unbiased and unrestrained service to its clients for both construction and maintenance work. This advice will reflect the practical experience of 75 years of service to sports clubs and the findings of the extensive programme of research which is carried out at the Institute. Furthermore, the consultancy services are supported by specialist soil physics, biology and soil chemistry laboratories.

Author's Note

In order that the information contained in this booklet may be presented for the benefit of readers in readily understandable fashion, it is in some cases necessary to use trade names to identify materials, machinery or equipment rather than complicated formulations or other lengthy descriptions. In doing so, it is unavoidable that in certain instances similar products which may be available under other trade names are not included. It should be noted that no endorsement of named products is implied or intended. Neither is the omission of any similar products to be taken as express or implied criticism.

Published 2006 by:

STRI, ST. IVES ESTATE, BINGLEY, WEST YORKSHIRE, BD16 1AU, ENGLAND

STRI disclaimer